Invitations from the Divine

Extraordinary Real Life Stories

DR. KAREN HANKS

"Walk slowly for there isn't very much time..."

Anonymous

ABOUT DR. KAREN

Karen has had a life surrounded by Angels, beings and animals that have kept her safe and feeling loved through life's losses and pain.

She has had the gift of listening to the Divine and following this guidance. This has lead her to great adventures, wonders, with people and animals, which she has been deeply grateful for and eternally in wonder of it all.

In the world she has studied horticulture, homeopathy, rock climbing, healing of many types for humans and animals, computer programming, diesel mechanics, opera singing, ballet, dowsing, painting, Native American traditions, hypnosis and horses, horses, horses.

Karen has her doctorate in chiropractic, and from this education decided to develop her own type of energy and neurologic remapping. She has had the amazing opportunity to work with many well-known horses and their trainers, as well as amazing people and other animals, hoping to bring a deeper healing and understanding to all beings.

Karen has two magical children and two amazing grandchildren. She lives in Arizona, off the grid, with her ancient Soul of a husband and a lovely menagerie of beings of all shapes and sizes, all of which bring daily wonder into her life.

Published by
Dr. Karen Hanks
P.O. Box 669,
Ash Fork, AZ 86320

For information regarding Consultations,
Treatment Sessions, Workshops,
Programs and Products, please contact
Dr. Karen at tinkerbellina@msn.com.

All the stories in this book are true.
Some names have been changed to
protect the privacy of individuals.

Cover feathers photo ©2016 Nadtytok/Shutterstock.
Cover light beams illustration ©2016 Eliks/Shutterstock.
Cover design by Yvonne Wilcox.

ISBN-13: 978-1541096134
ISBN-10: 1541096134

This book is not intended as a substitute for the medical advice of physicians. The reader should regularly consult a physician in matters relating to his/her health and particularly with respect to any symptoms that may require diagnosis or medical attention.

This book is dedicated to all of those who have a voice, with a body or without, four-legged, two-legged or other, who are waiting to be heard.

May we listen to you.

CONTENTS

Acknowledgments . . . . *vii*

Introduction *1*

1. A Son Returns. *5*
2. Eclipse, The Cat *14*
3. Time Bending *18*
4. ET's Among Us *21*
5. Kaitlyn's Angel *26*
6. What Our Bodies Can Show. *29*
7. Premonitions Of My Dad's Death *34*
8. Travels Of The Mind And Soul *40*
9. We. *43*
10. A Shared Past Life *45*
11. Dogs Talking. *50*
12. Special 'Talent'. *59*
13. Conner *66*
14. Grandmother Spider. *69*
15. Projecting. *72*
16. Horse Telepathy *79*
17. The Dog Who Said *"I Don't Like My Food"*. . . *86*
18. Guidance From A Native American Elder *91*
19. Falling In Love With A Pack Rat *97*
20. Dowsing For Lost Things *103*
21. Death *106*
22. A Dead Grandfather Returns To Help *110*
23. Cha Cha And Volcom, Blessed Dogs. *116*
24. You've Ruined My Life *121*
25. Mind Reading *126*
26. Ghosts *130*

ACKNOWLEDGEMENTS

I t seems that every author of every book I have ever read has the same dilemma: how to thank all who made this current work of art possible. I am a new hand at this but will give it a try.

I am in deepest honor and devotion to the Great One, Great Spirit, the Divine One, God and to all the beings who literally lent their wings to me when I had none, so that I would learn more and more to trust the Universe, the Great Divine, and all it had in its hands for me.

In giving thanks, I must always turn to my greatest non-bodied teachers first: Jesus, Holy Spirit, Angels (including my Ten-Thousand Angels), guides of all sorts, Ancient Ones who had passed and were willing to teach, including Buddha, and many others including all animal spirits and others with great wisdom which have held my hands and heart when times seemed dark.

I am also thankful to loved ones who have passed, who have given up their sacred body temple but not their Souls, who still love me from far and near and are there in my daily life, always helping me. I bow my head and heart to all of you, as without you I would not be here. I am full of your teachings and love which I offer to all who are

Divinely put in my path.

I am also in deepest gratitude for all of my bodied beloveds. My husband, Kenny Wayne, seems to make all things possible by causing me to check into, update, renovate, and preserve every part of my being by constantly drawing me into love and training me to live with higher and higher levels of mastery of loving. He would say, "Yes, Doll." I would say, "Thank you, Babe."

To Kaitlyn and Conner; Zen masters. I cannot even begin to tell you and show you how grateful I am that you both chose me to be your mom in this lifetime. Who gets this lucky? I guess I do; my head bowed to you both for the endless lessons in love with which you have gifted me and still do, daily. Thank you.

Kaitlyn, thank you for the gifts of self-awareness and grace. I have constantly stood in awe of you for these and more ever since you were little.

Conner, thank you for the gift of unending enthusiasm and never giving up on being yourself no matter how hard it is. Again, you have been a great teacher for me.

I am thankful for Tyler and Weston, magical beings growing up with a magical mommy. Again, I am in awe to be a part of it.

Thanks to my animal family: Buddy the magical dog, Volcom, Zero, Alex, Fred, the turtles, Razzo, Dillon, Jake, Lol, Classy, Sugar, Pumpkin, Rodney, Rusty, Bria, Sissy, Sofie, Tuxedo, Bowtie, Amber Lee, Audie, Johnnie Ringo and Curley Bill.

And much gratitude to all, all, all, all others who are in my life and who have helped make this happen.

Many, many thanks to Vonni for being the open door and the Divine blessing to midwife this book.

Thanks to my i-dotter and t-crosser and world traveling companion, Sheila; to the practical side of Spirit she will always ask the question for which we need an answer and make the straight-out comment. We love her for this!

Thanks to Cloud, my Spirit Mom since my birth mother across the rainbow bridge is without the arms to hug me in tough and happy times.

Thanks to all of my friends and clients and your animals.

To all the people and animals, including horses, along the way who have trusted me with their deepest hopes and dreams, secrets and wonders, I give you my deepest love and gratitude. Here is only a sampling of this group: Jane, Frosty, Jason, Abby, Marshall, Mark, Hela, Sheila, Liz, Leslie, Leslie, Barbara, Wayne, Jordan, Blair, Rascal, Tina, Ryan, Julie, Gabriella, Simonetta, Silvia, Daniela, Mila, Barbara, Giovanna, Edie, Elena, Pat and Linda, Caton, Westpoint, Dylano, Slider, Coconut, Vinnie and Moxie, Coco, Monty and Pat and Deborah and Colonial, Colleen and Saint, Luis, Luca, Patrick, Elna, Lynn, Emma, Kathleen and Cody, Kathy, Dale, Tina, Johnathan, Jamie, Bev, Lillan, Anna, Barry, Stinky, Sondra, Willie, Amber, Sharon, Flashy, Cooper, Dominque, and Deborah. I give you all my heartfelt thanks.

To all who I have been in service to in any way, thank you. With my head bowed and my hands in prayer over my heart. Thank you all.

A big huge 'Thank You' to the Divine and Vonni for the

creation of this book in real time.

I must share here that invitations from the Divine are often not easy, come with much resistance, and often seem completely the 'wrong' thing. Of course they do. If this invitation was NOT going to mold you, uplift you, clean you up, heal you, make you more of your Divine self, it would feel grand. Notice I said 'NOT.' If you were already all of these things, you already WOULD be all of these things. So, growth is scary and painful just as teething is painful. Yet for all the years of biting and eating, that pain is worth it. However, I would guess it doesn't seem so in the moment. In the moment, I imagine all of us would do anything not to have this happen. We can't stop teething, however we can stop this type of growing and growth later on, and we do, all of the time.

So the Divine created a very uncomfortable container for Vonni and I. And I believe because I love her so much and can peek behind the veil of the way things APPEAR and the way they actually ARE, I trusted. She trusted me, too. And her offering was to help me write a book; this book. Who would have known, from that crazy uncomfortable, disconnected communication place, that this is what God had in mind?

Now, this could have gone in any direction for both of us, but it is my belief that in the middle of great disconnect, aloneness, misunderstanding and brace, is the emotional compost for wonder, magic and healing.

You just need to keep trusting. Do what the Divine asks, no more and no less, and wait for it, with no attachment, only love and an open heart.

So, thank you, Vonni, for all the magic you bring, not only to me and this book but to all who will hopefully share in its joy and wonder.

– from Vonni

Getting to work on this book with Dr. Karen was truly an invitation from the Divine. We had not ever discussed working together on a project before, but a series of unexpected events caused us to have a conversation we might never had otherwise had.

This book wanted to be written! I have never before seen words and stories come together so quickly, and have never before felt so guided when helping an author put together their book.

Getting to read the stories as they came through has had quite an impact in my day-to-day life. These stories have helped me to feel calmer and to have a sense of 'knowing' that there truly is more to what we see and experience. But best of all, my fears have been replaced with a sense of safety and security, knowing that we can always "Ask..."

Thank you Dr. Karen, and thank you to the Divine, for an invitation we couldn't refuse :)

* * *

To You, Dear Beloved One,

If you are reading this, welcome to your Invitation from the Divine! Welcome home! This book is for you! Hopefully it will gently and sweetly whisper in your ear and your Soul what you might have forgotten about yourself, the Divine One, and life here on planet Earth.

And again, welcome! It has been too long since we have seen you and been able to hug you. We are so happy you are back here with us, *Home.*

INTRODUCTION

They are speaking, will we listen?

In the arms of the everywhere we are held. We are never alone, never without guidance and love, not only from our Great Creator, but from every brother and sister near us, next to us, and far away from us.

There is never a far away, not any away for that matter.

We humans forget so much. We forget that we are all tethered together, woven into one particle that cannot turn away from itself, as we are all 'Godstuff.'

The same stuff that is the dog, tree, rock, sofa, is the stuff of us, too, and is connected in ways we can't even begin to imagine. All are breathing the same air. The trees, bees and humans.

We can track the earth's history in the particles of memory she carries in her air. I am breathing you, and you are breathing me. We are breathing the air all of the beings on the planet have breathed – forever. We are all breathing each other. The same is true for the water that is us, the water that creates for us in our bodies, and the water that we drink.

We are an amazing Soul destination, a contained planet that is a theatre where Souls grow and school; a place where we can act out any theatre story we wish and then return to our Great gathering place, Heaven, to remember and integrate what we have learned.

We can laugh with the Souls we killed or hurt as it was a theatre piece here on earth, like a Disney movie or cruise where tragedy happens in the first five minutes of the movie and the rest is working towards a happily ever after. Then a good laugh and gratefulness to the beings that allowed you tragic deaths, huge emotional wounds, grief, and loss.

All of these are the illusions of the earth theatre. Even us forgetting our true Soul selves with only glimmers, seeking to find this again too, is the purpose of this theatre and ultimately how we learn to love more.

It is always about how to love more; more deeply and thoroughly, more vastly and creatively, in very deep ways, as we drop the veil/curtain we have created. In this earth theater and our other spirit worlds, we receive a glimmer of the purpose and understanding.

We can hear all the Souls of the Spirits talking in their ways to us. Or in their ways they must change, make a huge effort to change their speak enough so that we might hear/see and understand.

We are never without help in our earth theatre walk. Ancestors, Angels, animal guides, both in bodies and without bodies, trees, earth rocks, grass, insects, flowers, mushrooms, on and on. The Divine One never wants or wanted us to suffer in our theatre story. There are always places to turn to for help. This, too, is part of our Soul's growth.

It is my prayer that the stories in this book are a door into the beautiful wisdom, teaching and gifts that I received by being a part of each story. May they be such a gift to you.

There is no mistake that you have picked up this book and are reading it. Maybe somehow it picked you. The Divine in it knew your Soul was ready to hear them speaking, and now you are ready to hear.

These are but a sampling of stories that have been gifted into my personal life. It is also my prayer that in some way you, too, will hear the bigger call and that you are a beloved one in this great family of beings you might not have considered related to you, until now. Maybe you have known this all along, and will smile as the stories sing to your heart.

May I welcome you home, Dear Cousin. May I help you remember with the help of these Spirits what you may have forgotten.

Many, many blessings always,

Karen

A SON RETURNS

Once, while working in Italy, a married couple came to me whose son had died. I remember him to have been in his early twenties; a baby in Italy. He was their first born and they also had a daughter who was in her teens. They told me the children had been best friends and deep confidants to each other. The son had not been feeling well and they could not awaken him one morning. They took him to the hospital and shortly after he was pronounced dead.

The doctors had no idea as to the cause of his death. These parents were in deep pain. First, their son had died suddenly. Second, it was mysterious, seeming without any reason; he was a healthy boy. Third, many thought the parents were lying and that he had died of a drug overdose. This caused them even more pain in the loss of their son, as this was not the case. The doctors were clear he had not died of this cause. They just could not determine what the cause was.

So, here they were. They had heard about me and were hoping to get some answers, some relief from their pain. Something, anything, that would help them live again, especially for their daughter, even if they couldn't manage it completely for themselves.

They had scheduled two sessions, one for each of them. I was clearly and Divinely told to keep them together. I had never done a session with two people together before, so this was a deep act of faith and I would need to rely deeply on my translator Daniela to catch all of the nuances of what might need to be translated from the Angels and hopefully from their son.

So… we started. What did they believe? Did they believe that their son could talk with them? That he was always near, watching? Did they believe in Angels? Guardian Angels? What about God? Were they mad at him? What were their true deep hopes, barriers and concerns?

The next layer opened. They had always believed, were Catholic, and didn't know what to think about possibly 'talking' to their son. Was that okay? Against him? Or God? Yes, they believed in Angels and, of course, Guardian Angels.

The father finally spoke up in a deeper concern that he didn't believe that this would work and really came for his wife. They both were suffering, but he didn't believe, so if I could do something for her, anything, that would be what they hoped. But they did not expect for anything to happen.

"Okay," I said. "So if we can put all judgement aside about any beliefs you have, let me ask, have you felt your son at all? Has he tried to make any contact with you that you really felt was him?" "Yes," they both said though the translator. "So, tell me what this was." "Four-leaf clover," they said; again, all translated. I smiled at my translator Daniela, already knowing that this Divine Appointment for me was full of this dead son trying to get in touch with his parents.

I was charmed.. Hmmm, one four-leaf clover. I loved this

boy already. "How many have you seen?" I asked, knowing that the father had told me he was a skeptic all along. "Hundreds," they said.

"What?" I said, "Hundreds of four-leaf clovers since he died and you don't think he has been trying to contact you?"

They both laughed and the father said, "Yes." Even after hundreds he wasn't convinced, although the mother said she knew it, and went on to say when she was pregnant with her son they also found four-leaf clovers everywhere; that she had rarely found even one in the past, but when she was pregnant she and they seemed to find them so often that they couldn't believe it. It became a symbol of only good things about this child.

The father then said, "Well, I was a bit convinced that my son was trying to say something, or was near, when one night after his death we were out walking and a letter landed at my wife's feet. It was blowing around, we saw it, then it landed at her feet. We decided to pick it up and put it back in the post, but we couldn't bring ourselves to do that. We feel embarrassed to this day, but we felt we had to open it. It was a letter written by an old woman to her old friend. She talked about what was happening in her life and said that she was sending the friend a small gift. When we saw what it was we couldn't believe it. It was the biggest four leaf-clover we had ever seen. Pressed and saved and sent, my wife felt, from our son."

I too, could not deny this. This felt too strange, unusual, unexplainable, for it not to be their son trying to reach them and tell them something. Again, I smiled, "Yes! He has been with you all along trying to comfort you."

The father again mentioned that he never imagined life without his son, how his whole life was about him dying first, that his son would be with him when he was old, with his sister when she married, and again, if only he could get some comfort for his wife who had been telling some of the story but mostly weeping.

I asked them to get comfortable, to lie down. They chose to lie at ninety degrees to each other with feet near, and heads away. I sat between them and would move back and forth to each one as needed.

I called the Guardian Angels and asked if it was possible and appropriate for their son to share some time with his parents, and for them to be able to ask any questions on their hearts, to understand the answers, and what it meant to them; for them to receive whatever they needed to be able to move through this time.

And so it began.

The Mom felt and saw her son right away. I asked her to talk with him and ask any questions she wished, and told her if she needed help to let me know. She cried, but now it was because she could see him and talk with him. She seemed to settle in, as if her son, in his body, had just walked in the room. Her whole posture changed as she smiled and cried and relaxed.

Dad, however, seemed tense, maybe even irritated, stiff and resistant. I asked how he was doing. Nothing. 'Hmmm,' I thought, 'his child is here.' I prayed for more help. 'Please let him receive what he needs.' Mom continued, almost cooing now, happy and cooing.

Suddenly, Dad's arm lifted, as if someone took hold of his hand, and gently raised his arm into the strangest position. Daniela kept translating in my soft tone, meanwhile pointing in disbelief at the position of the father's arm and hand. It just hung there, and hung there, and hung there. Other worldly, it hung there in a position no human could hold that long, much less unsupported. We were amazed how comfortable and happy this father looked, eyes closed for at least an hour, with his arm twisted in the oddest way I have ever seen, hanging in the air.

I gave them as much time as they both wanted to share with their son, letting them know they could visit with him at anytime – that this was a beginning and not an end. They relaxed into a different position and opened their eyes, feeling completely different than when they had arrived.

The mother said that her son shared many things with her; that they had talked and talked. The father, now the quiet, thought-filled one, listened to what his wife was sharing, waiting for the translation to me and then back to them. Then there was a pause, a quiet, and the father said, "I believe. My son came to me and held my hand. I felt him come beside me and hold my hand. Everything has changed for me now."

Daniela and I asked him in which position he felt his son hold his hand. He showed us and said, "I could not have held it that way if my son had not held it for me." We all agreed.

Thoughtfully and with deep gratitude we all felt blessed to have shared time with this couple's Divine son.

– from Daniela, the translator

(Please note, some details differ, but we have included them exactly as each person recalled.)

I remember that you were wearing a very fancy top (would say with some green) and high heels and this of course it is the most important part of the story .. LOL ! ;)

I remember that the wife and husband had booked for two sessions and they asked if they could have a joint one. When they entered the room (the big space of the Shiatsu school), they were actually clinging to each other as they were just one person ...

At the beginning they started talking about their son. His name was Stephano. They were saying he was kind of a rebel and not always easy to persuade in doing things. He was not much interested in school but was very special in the way he dealt with people.

I remember that you told them that he was saying to you "Sorry I did not see it arriving" and they explained that one morning he was found dead in his bed. They thought he could have taken some drugs and they said that his body went under autopsia (I don't remember if he was tested positive or negative though, but I have a feeling he was negative and this lifted some blame out of his death.

You were explaining to them that you had witnessed many cases like them and although it is painful they could be ensured that they are going to be rejoined in spirit and that he had just gone ahead and will be welcoming them when it will be the time. These young souls are often special souls and are allowed to stay with us for certain amount of time but nevertheless they are a gift.

They shared that before Stephano's departure they were not believing in God and anything related to spirit or a life after death. This is because they were grown as active politically and against the church. However, after Stephano's departure they started to open up to this possibility.

You have asked whether they have been receiving some messages from him and they told us the story of the four-leaf clover.

She has started to find clover everywhere in the most incredible places. It happened so many times that she started feeling it could not be considered a simple coincidence. So every time she was finding one, she was telling herself that this might be a sign from Stephano.

Then, one summer night they were walking together at night and a certain point a letter was blown by the wind and hit their feet. They gathered it and joking to one another, they started saying "let's see who has written us tonight."

They also felt bad about opening the letter, but they were also curious and were drawn to do it.

When they opened the letter they were stunned. In fact there was a very intimate letter (I believe of friendship but I don't remember if it was from a woman to a man or between two women) and in the envelope the sender was sending two huge four-leaf clovers!

At that stage we were all weeping. She said that she was missing him a lot and her biggest desire was to be able to dream about him so that she could see his face again. You suggested that she may lay down and see if it would be possible for her to perceive him with your help. You first asked with a silent prayer and then were keeping your fingers on her forehead on the third chakra to try to overcome his fears and allow the experience to take place.

The husband also laid down almost at 90 degrees from his wife. You told them that Stephano was already in the room.

Then, for a long time there was only silence, I could see tears going down from her face and at the same time I started noticing that the hand of the father slowly moving and slowly by slowly raising up and then floating in the air.

I remember that the physical experience of this arm was for Stephano's father a life-changing experience. Before that there have been words and hopes after there was a tangible proof.

Stephano knew he was skeptical and had to do something BIG. When his arm started floating all his doubts and resistance dropped and he was able to accept and understand all other moments of the past in which Stephano was trying to break through his resistances.

We were glad that they shared the session as they both were kind of changed by it and when they walked out from the room they seemed further intimate and bonded, if possible, than when they had arrived ...

Blessing:

This was an incredible story of love as well as how much we can resist or not be sure about a loved one who has transitioned and is trying to communicate with us. I loved that this young man was so determined to communicate with his parents.

Offering:

When you think loved ones who have passed (including animals) are with you or trying to communicate with you (even in dreams), please open to them even more. Say 'yes' to how they are trying to send you love and messages from where they are standing, right next to you, (without a body). Allow it and notice and smile as I hope you will feel very loved as they connect and stay with and by you.

ECLIPSE, THE CAT

This happened many years ago before it was popular, when most people didn't even know about animal communicating.

I decided to take a class from a woman who had been trained by a very famous Animal Communicator who came from England. I took this wonderful class and felt fairly accomplished after the class had ended; maybe even a bit proud of myself.

That said, at that time I had a cat named Eclipse who would meow and meow and meow and meow to go out every morning. The first thing the morning after the class had ended was no exception. My daughter and I were living on a very busy five-pointed intersection that had had many accidents on it; enough so that when we moved into the home there was someone killed on the corner on the first night we were there. It was strange because I was a doctor on this corner, so there was a little bit of a local joke about having an accident on the corner and wandering into my office dazed and confused, only to meet up with my receptionist. The place was very well known at the local police department.

So there sat my cat at the door meowing and meowing and

meowing to go out. I was always terrified that she would be squished during these hours. The rest of the time the streets were completely quiet, except for the morning and evening commute which were the times she wanted to go out!

There she sat, face to the door, trying to go out. So I decided to use my new animal communication skills on her, and for sure I figured I would get through. My teacher had taught me to think the thought that I wanted to send in as much detail as possible. Describing it, or seeing and visualizing it in my mind, then opening the doors of my heart and sending it out.

There I stood, with her not even glancing at me, imagining her first getting hit by a car and sending this out to her. Sending it and sending it, that she would be hit by a car, which is why I didn't want to open the door and let her out.

There was no reaction from her at all. It was really crazy how I was working so hard and she just kept her face to the door, not even paying any attention to me, just meowing and meowing and meowing.

I decided to up my game as my teacher had taught, and with as much terrible, terrible, terrible visualization as I could, I visualized her getting hit on the road, with body parts and blood everywhere and the car dragging her down the road. I visualized images of everything violent and terrible that I could imagine in my biggest fears. Then I really, really, really pushed this visualization out through my heart and to her. Still she just sat looking at the door, ignoring me, not even turning around.

I tried this for what seemed like many, many, many minutes, probably fifteen or twenty. (I'm sure it wasn't that long, but it seemed like forever.) Finally I decided it wasn't working at all, I was a terrible communicator and I couldn't believe I felt at all even the slightest bit accomplished.

I turned to walk away from her, and did not get one step before I heard a voice from behind me that was a voice I had never heard in my entire life. It was a gravelly, smoky kind of voice that said, "Don't you think I can take care of myself?!"

When I turned around Eclipse was looking at me, eyes huge and very annoyed. Of course I walked over, opened the door, and let her out.

Blessing:

My blessing from this experience was to have the realization just how hard it must have been for Eclipse to have been so misunderstood. Every day all of my interactions with her were from my misguided ideas and then misguided conclusions about her. I made my world around her about how to correct her behavior or how to prevent her or save her from herself. All of this came from being driven from an incredibly incorrect belief about her and her life and actions. I treated her from the perspective that she was in a way dumb because I was so convinced from my human point of view about what I believed about her. This all changed immediately when I heard her speak to me.

Offering:

Is there any animal in your life for which you have a deep belief about his or her behavior which might come from you believing something about that animal that really is not true? How can you start to open to another perspective? Can you perhaps ask your animal for more information? How might this change your ideas about animals in general and how they are behaving?

TIME BENDING

It was a beautiful day in Rome, Italy and my friend Silvia and I were going to go to the sea. As I remember, this was a very crowded day and our timing seemed to be not so good inasmuch that the first part of the train ride was delayed.

As we got off at the first station to catch the next train, which was not very frequent to go to the sea, it seemed as though hundreds of people were scrambling and we were late. I, being originally from the East Coast, quickened my pace to rush in front of all of these folks to see if we could get the train before it left.

My friend Silvia is a Tai Chi Master and Chi Gong Master. In my rushing, as Sylvia would, she gently touched my hand and told me to slow down. A slow-down for me is maybe half pace of a very fast walk. She just smiled and started walking in the most slow and precise way.

To me it seemed as if she was not walking at all, and in this slow, beautiful walking we became a bubble to each other and I saw people quickly passing us by. Faces passing by, and yet she and I walked slowly with great intention and incredible happiness. We truly, I felt, were in a bubble all our own. At that moment I didn't care if we made the train or not as I was with my friend Silvia, a master, and a person whom I love so much. Cares faded and just huge love surrounded me.

We arrived at the door of the train. There were just a few people inside and I noticed the people who had passed us, rushing, were now behind us. Let me say that again: We arrived at the door with only a few lazy, comfortable people in the train and as we stopped at the door, the people who had passed us were now behind us!

We stepped onto the train. I smiled, knowing I'm always cared for, pondering Sylvia's ability again. I had experienced the portal she created in space and time that comfortably, lovingly, easily carried us to our destination.

– from Silvia

I thought back to the episode about the train ... I do not remember exactly when it was, but it's a situation I know well and I have lived so many times ... Especially here in Rome were people live in such a frantic and crazy way! I often see people running fast, always anxious to get. I watch them going around in circles... Why do they run and run?

Sometimes it's so easy and relaxing to slow down, changing pace is a chance to change perspective, open an horizon and see far away. Like in that train, we got there in time anyway, and there was a nice place for us, too! And all that useless rush behind us... Just waiting sometimes brings unexpected rewards!

Blessing:

This experience brought me many blessings as it still does to this day. There is the blessing of listening to a master, a guide, and how comforting this can be when someone can notice something and truly help you, and that they offer from the heart to do that. Another blessing was the gift of remembering how to 'bend' time. Time often seems our enemy, but perhaps it is because we are not in the dance with him or her properly. Also a blessing that came from this is what is ours is ours to receive; there is no rush. Stay mindfully and peacefully on your path, offering an open heart and all is always well. Better than well.

Offering:

Next time (or any time) you are aware of not being present, feeling the need to hurry or rush, slow down and then slow down more and see what blessings you receive and what magic happens.

ET'S AMONG US

As a young woman I had moved to North Carolina. I was going to college and living in a bread truck which was parked in a campground where some people lived year-round and some seasonally.

For me this was a wondrous place. The man who owned it had been a deep-sea diver and his office was full of pictures of the sea. He even had his deep-sea diving suit, helmet, and all his diving equipment in his office. He was an older gentleman and just talking to him was a blessing.

This place was in the woods and everyone who lived there seemed a bit magical or wondrous to me, so coming home from school and work felt like coming home to a Hobbit-like adventure. I was always excited.

There was a photographer who lived in this campground and he and I became friends. He needed someone to do some modeling, so I modeled for him as he photographed me for some business advertising. He also filmed me for a local Toyota commercial which sadly, though beautifully filmed, never made it to television.

One early afternoon I was invited into his little camper area. I felt a bit awkward for although he and I had known each other for a while, I had never been in his living space. When I walked in I became even more uncomfortable because there were black and white pictures all over the upper portion of this trailer, all of women.

The inside of my body began to get tight as I felt very uncomfortable with all of these women in his small space. The conversation went from him telling me about Transcendental Meditation (I was also uncomfortable about that at that time as I had been raised in a very religious setting) to me mustering up a sparkly, "Look at all of these pictures of these women… Did you photograph all of them?"

His face darkened. I was really unsure at that moment what was coming next. With a solemn face he said, "These are all pictures of one woman, who is my teacher." I looked back at the pictures. All of the women were so different looking; they were young and old. I could not believe it was the same woman. Then inside myself I rested with the thought that, okay, these were just pictures of a person's whole lifetime.

He saw me studying the pictures, and with great reverence, as you would tell a story about your most beloved treasured memory, he started, "This is my teacher. She is a walk-in."

He saw my face change and knew he needed to explain. "She is a walk-in; an extraterrestrial. There was this twenty-year-old woman who wanted to commit suicide. She made a spiritual agreement with my teacher where instead of killing herself, she would lie down on a bridge, let her Spirit leave her body, and my teacher's Spirit would walk in to be able to be here on Earth to accomplish teaching and help us."

Inside I was reeling. I had never heard of anything like this before. Suddenly it felt as if the pictures had come alive and this woman was staring at me from every direction, from every very different manifestation of who she was.

He continued: "The young woman who left her body on the bridge and the new soul that entered her is now my teacher. She came to teach us many things. The group she started teaching became larger and larger as the things she told us we knew to be true. This information changed us. We prospered and saw life from a very different perspective. The group became more and more empowered and she taught more and more. However, at some point, people seemed to begin to worship her – and this was not her purpose. She was very clear with us that this was not our purpose. So she told us she had to leave us because we were not understanding her purpose. She explained she would demonstrate for us that she would age twenty years within just a few years. She would go into business and manifest millions of dollars to show us what she was saying and teaching us was true. She would also show us what, through the pain of us behaving towards her as a savior, we had actually lost."

Again, I was stunned as I looked around at these photographs. I could see this woman had gone from a beautiful, young, vibrant twenty-something year-old to a woman in her thirties or forties looking very businesslike and very changed, and full of unhappiness or sadness. The more her life took the course of ours in the way we all live here on Earth, the more unhappy, or bound, or sad she became, even though she was fabulously wealthy.

I must have been staring at these pictures for a long time, because he told me it was time to leave. I felt now as if her story was written on my heart, so I said to him, "Where is she now? Do you still keep in touch with her? What's going on now?"

He answered, "Yes, every now and then. But she's doing what she said she would do to prove to us more about ourselves and how we are."

As I stepped out of the trailer, he added "...and she knows you, too, Karen. She knows you, too, and she'll contact you when the time is right."

I can't even tell you where I was emotionally with all of this. I pondered it. I felt overwhelmed by it. I knew he absolutely believed this. I did not know if I could believe it but it really stayed in my heart.

About two-and-a-half years passed and I had moved away from that campground. I was living by myself in an apartment for the first time, working three jobs and going to school. Life was busy and consuming.

One day I drove up to the post office in my little VW Bug to pick up my mail. I hadn't picked up my mail in some time so there was a huge amount of it. So I was sitting in my car on a sunny, beautiful day with the window part-way down. I was looking down at my lap full of mail when I felt someone looking at me.

I looked up, and it was this woman. It felt like she was just inches from my face with her head in the window of my VW. She was smiling at me and waited until I recognized her.

Then she winked at me and walked away.

Blessing:

Since this story spanned a few years, I believe it was one, as many in my life, that felt like a seed was planted to receive its proper nourishment later to grow and sprout.

Earlier in my life as a teen, a group of friends and I had an encounter with seeing and following a UFO. It seems to me that there is always a long thread that we can follow through our lives as our Soul and Spirit are weaving the stories we write on our Souls. So, the blessing from this story was very deep and there is so much that is beyond me.

So much I may never know, but can be a part of my life AND that I might be a part of, even if I don't know why.

Offering:

Where is, or has there been, wonder in your life that was an event for which you had no reference? Maybe you can cherish it as an act of wonder and grace and a not-knowing the why, that might be a thread that gets woven into your future, like... "To be continued," in your life.

KAITLYN'S ANGEL

My daughter was about three years old; that beautiful age where they are talking about everything that only parents, grandparents and savvy language dissectors can understand. They are aware of everything in their world and talking about it.

At the time I was a single mom, separated from my husband. My daughter and I lived in a beautiful rental in New Hope, Pennsylvania. I was a young doctor and my practice was in the front of the house that we rented on the river.

My daughter Kaitlyn and I were enjoying some time together in the big back room of the house, the room that faced the river, when my daughter said, "Look Mommy!" I looked and did my mom smile, trying to acknowledge something I didn't really see or understand – yet. I was hoping I would catch onto it soon, before she realized I had no idea what she was pointing to or talking about.

"Look Mommeeee... Look!" She kept pointing to the same area in the window. I saw nothing inside or outside. She was catching on that I didn't see it. "Look," she said harder.

"Mommy is looking, Sweetie. I don't see it. I'm sorry. Tell

me what you see." She looked like I was kidding her, then she realized I wasn't.

"Don't you see it Mommy? Don't you see it? It's riiiigggght there." She pointed more exacting than ever before, and with her arm held up, finger pointing, she looked at me, certain I would see it, disbelieving that I couldn't.

"No Sweetheart, I don't see it."

Now teary, she said, "Mommy, you don't see the baby right there? The baby with wings right there? Mommy, look. I know you can see it. The baby with wings is right there.. Looking at us, right... theerre."

She started to cry. I said, "Oh Sweetie, I am so sorry! Sometimes children see things that when we grow up and become adults we no longer can see. That doesn't mean they are not real, just that adults have lost the ability to see them."

"Mommy, you can't see the baby with wings?"

"No, I can't see her," I said. "I wish I could." My daughter rushed into my arms and cried and cried. I cried and cried too.

The baby with the wings that my daughter saw was a baby Angel. She knew nothing of these as she was too young. However, she knew everything of these as she saw with her own eyes one who came to visit, floating in our room by the window, as real as everything she had ever experienced.

Blessing:

Even I, who sees all sorts of things others don't see; even

I, could not see this particular Angel. At the moment it felt cruel, maybe even more cruel, because I do see so much and not being able to see it so deeply hurt my daughter. This said, it was an amazing gift. The person in front of me saw and was in the presence of an Angel. I was too, I just couldn't 'see' this baby with wings. Was it any less real? Was I not a part of the blessing even though I didn't 'see' it? No. And so I, in review, fell in love with being in the presence of a miracle, even if I/we don't see it, feel it, IT is still happening and I am here with it.

To receive a miracle, no matter what my judgement that might take me away from the miracle, is big. For me to open to the bigger, beyond me, beyond my human definition of what this miracle or miracles 'should' look like. I am not God, (although at this moment I am behaving like God with this sort of judgement and criticalness). How could I do this and how could I invalidate what was being given to me in such a precious way; in this case with and through my daughter.

So, my big lesson is to smile, open, love it, say thank you, and be so so so grateful, at every little (which is always big, there is another judgement) magic, miracle.

Offering:

Stop or suspend your judgement about all of the miracles that are happening around you that you dismiss. There are no coincidences. God is in every thing. So, smile and receive it, deep into your heart.

WHAT OUR BODIES CAN SHOW

While in my practice, I had many people who were survivors of some type of abuse and because I was doing energy work and balancing the body, it was really helping people to start remembering clearly their abuse; what had been hidden by their subconscious mind to protect them. Their bodies remembered until their minds were safe enough to reveal to them the clear memory of that time. To say my practice at that time was very particular and peculiar would have been a mild description.

Often when a client was new and filling out paperwork, another client in another room would be screaming, and I mean screaming. (Sometimes as the body remembers, a client will relive parts of what happened to them in the way that their body and mind have logged it, so once again it can be horrible. That said, we always hope to create a safe place to re-experience that horror.) My receptionist would calmly smile at the new client and say, "Don't worry, soon that will be you," always keeping her smile.

At some moment in time a patient called and asked to be alone in the office with me. Although there were clients who wished to have more privacy, this request was the first of its kind.

The day came when this client who had asked for total privacy showed up. It turned out that she had been a sexual abuse therapist as well as a death and dying therapist. She had been sending many clients to me because of my success in helping them remember their past abuse. Now she was ready to try for herself.

She had told me that she had been in the business for many years and had been trying unsuccessfully for over seventeen years to remember what happened to her as a child. She knew she had been sexually abused, as at some moment in time nearly 100% of the patients in my practice had been. I was her last hope and she didn't want any of her clients to see her there working with me.

We started our work together and it did not take long until signs of her abuse started showing up. The first sign was her calling me after about the fourth or fifth treatment. On her way home she felt burning on her legs that started to show up all over her body. She started investigating further and found what looked like welts that came from someone hitting her with something. She came into the office to show them to me. They were the most bizarre expression of abuse I had ever seen. There were huge open wounds all over her body, as if someone had hit her with a whip. There was a line in the middle and welts on either side, as if it had just happened, on her back legs and almost everywhere on her body.

I laughed, as she did too, because we knew we were touching some place in her and her body was speaking, even though she had no memory yet.

In the days and treatments that followed, the most amazing thing would happen to both of us. It was a moment when she was in my treatment room, face down, and all of a sudden she shrieked. It was like we were in a 'Star Wars' movie where a hologram of Obi-Wan Kenobi showed up on her lower back area. A scene unfolded in front of me of incredible abuse and terror. I watched as if in 3D the movie played off of her back.

She told me afterwards that she could not speak. She had remembered what had happened and I told her that she didn't need to tell me, because I had seen it. We would later talk about these moments, but in the meantime, she needed some time to heal.

On her next visit we sat and shared what we both had seen and what she had remembered. We both saw that she was in a dark basement area and there were people around who were devil worshippers. She not only had been married to the devil in a ceremony, but had witnessed babies being killed as sacrifices. She had been raped when she was a very little girl and it looked to me as though her parents were part of this process, willingly allowing all of this to happen to her. She acknowledged that this was the truth.

In the months that followed I didn't see her for some time, then one day she came in and just scheduled time to talk. She had always kept her daughter away from her parents, as she felt that something was really wrong about them. After uncovering these memories, she decided to go home and confront her mother about what she remembered. At that time her parents were elderly and still lived in the home with the basement where she believed those rituals were performed.

As she went to leave after the visit with her mother, she got up the nerve to say something. As she was walking out the door she told me she turned to her mother and said, "I remember what you did to me as a child."

She told me that her mother's face went cold and she started pressing against the door as if to close it and keep her inside. Her mother then said, "Dear, does anyone know where you are?"

Blessing:

It seems for a very long time I have been able to 'see' a lot of different things around and in peoples', animals' and others' bodies. I have seen colors, aura, past lives, pain, people in their energy fields who have hurt them and really loved them, people and animals who have had a story in their lives.

This experience made all of this go even deeper for me. That connection to the projection being given off and the simultaneous awareness of the remembering or coming conscious of the story (again,) from where it has been locked and hidden, really amazed me.

Usually I am sharing with the living one what I am sensing and feeling; in this case to experience it when it was happening, again was remarkable and an incredible gift. That said, it also stops me in my tracks a bit for the affirmation of what is so readily available, in our bodies and energy fields, AND how deeply ALWAYS it/we are crying to be healed.

Offering:

Please know that you have access to these places in your-self, always. It usually is about getting quiet and safe enough to be able to receive what is always able and waiting to be delivered to you. So if there is a place in your life, a dark-ness, a wound, an unforgotten place or time, try being quiet, silent, safe. Slowing down enough that it can and might 'catch' you.

PREMONITIONS OF MY
DAD'S DEATH

I am an only child of older parents. My mom gave birth to me when she was forty after having two devastating miscarriages, so my parents were very happy to have me.

When I was about eleven, I started having premonitions.

These premonitions were particularly disturbing because they were visions of something I knew, beyond a shadow of a doubt, was going to happen. They were not dreams like people dream that something bad will happen, they were gifts (what I see now as gifts, but not then) of what was to come around my father. My dad was a joyful man, full of life, who awakened the goodness in everyone he met. I started seeing pictures and understanding that my dad would be dying soon.

When Robert Kennedy was assassinated there were pictures in my dad's Newsweek magazine of Robert's head, face away, in a pool of blood. My Dad looked a lot like Robert Kennedy. I was told, and understood, beyond any shadow of a doubt, that this would be the last way I would see my father, in a pool of blood.

When this overwhelming feeling was so present and ongoing, I prayed (my family was very religious) to God every prayer

I could pray. "Please don't take my father, please take me instead, don't leave me with my mother alone." But the feeling was overwhelming that my dad would be dying soon.

One afternoon my dad came to me, a big smile on his face as he stood in our hallway. I remember the light beaming from their bedroom into the hall. He looked at me and said, "I have no idea why I'm doing this, but my watch broke, and I was wondering if you might want it?" He looked at me with curiosity – why would anyone want a broken watch and why would he be offering it? But there was some kind of a light around him and I heard a voice as clear as any other voice on any other day say to me, "This will be the last thing your father gives you." (I believed this voice to be the voice of an Angel, who was near me.)

I was only eleven, so I had no capacity, understanding, or guidance; nothing except the very deep and real under-standing that this was what was happening to me. This information was more real than anything I ever knew and it seemed I had no power to change it.

Time went on, but not very long (I couldn't tell you how many days) until one morning I was working on finishing a school project. I was in the fifth grade and I was a terrible student in the way I left everything until the last minute. I was working on some fabulous project that I don't think children create anymore for fifth grade assignments, and was feeling a lot of pressure to hurry and complete this assign-ment, which was due that day.

I was sitting at my desk in my room which had a window facing the steps that went to the back porch of our house. My dad was in the bathroom right next to my room, shaving.

There was only one bathroom for the whole house, and I couldn't resist going into the bathroom as he would always play games with me while he was shaving. We laughed and laughed, and apparently made enough noise that it woke my mother. She sniped at us from the other side of the wall of the bathroom and said, "Be quiet, you two are being too loud and making too much noise and it's keeping me up."

My dad and I laughed in a hushed tone and continued the conjuring, poking and teasing in a much quieter way so my mother could go back to sleep.

Finally, my dad was done with his shaving and was ready to go out for his morning run. (My dad was the only person I knew who ran. When I was eleven, he would run two to three miles every morning for his health, and do the exercises he did when he was in the military. He was cutting edge.) I went back into my room, probably ten steps from the bathroom, and my dad went out the back door, another two steps from my bedroom, to the back hall and down the outside stairs (I thought).

As he went out the door, I heard him kick the can off the porch that my mother used to feed the birds. I thought nothing of it as my project had engulfed me, and I only had moments to finish it before I would be on my way to school.

I had worked and worked all morning with my head in this project, until my mother said, "Where's your father? His car is still here. Hasn't he gone to work yet?" Then a look came over her face and with great seriousness she said, "Let's go out the front door." So we started for the front door then she changed her mind and said, "No, let's go out the back door." I trailed behind her past the front door, through the kitchen to where we opened the back door; the door that was right by my bedroom, two steps from my bedroom door.

As we stepped out onto the very small back porch, there was my dad, at the bottom of the stairs, in a huge pool of blood, dead. The picture I had been shown flashed through my mind. There he was, facing away from me, dark hair contrasting in the deep crimson color of the huge pool of blood. The metal snow shovel stored for winter at the bottom of the stairs had cut the back of his head open.

'No!' I screamed on the inside, but I knew no matter how many bargains I was making with God right now, like, 'It's okay if he's in a wheelchair and can't do anything...' 'Please let him be alive...,' I knew... I could hear my mother screaming that my father was dead.

I turned one step back into our tiny house that my dad had built for his parents with his own money; the one that we moved into from our even tinier home when my grandmother died. I picked up the phone, dialed the local emergency number, told the person on the other end we needed help, gave directions, and went and stood at the end of the driveway by the mailbox so the police and ambulance could find us on our little rural dirt road.

The police and rescue people came and I just stood there. I never did see my father's face again, except at the funeral where it did not seem like my father's face at all.

The newspapers were happy to report that this man in his mid-fifties died of exercising too much. We were told that he died of a heart attack; a blood clot that had been released from his leg that hit his heart so suddenly, that he was dead before he hit the ground only a few steps away.

Years later we found out that my dad, who was an electrical lineman for public service, had been electrocuted. It had been enough that all who were working with him thought he was dead, as he "should have been," we were told. But he survived (only to die about two weeks later after being given a clean bill of health by the MD's just days before).

Somehow, somewhere along the way, my eleven-year-old self must have told someone that I knew that my dad was going to die. In my memory, whether it's true or not, when we finally went back to church without my dad, the minister walked down the aisle of this ancient, two-hundred-plus-year-old church and talked about being selfish if you knew that someone was going to die; that you had contributed to that person's death and were somehow involved with the devil.

I can truly say that all these years later I'm still haunted by that, as I believe this was a gift from heaven so that I could help my mother, who later told me she heard the voice of an Angel say, "He is dead, go out the back door."

Blessing:

This one I have worked on for years and years. From where I am in life now, it was a blessing to know how and about when my dad would die, and for my mother to have been told, too, in that moment. It is all of the other stuff that goes along with it that was really difficult to overcome.

First, the whys: "Why him, why now, why in this way, why can't it be changed, why can't it be easier, why God, why?"

Then the hows and what-ifs: "How will I deal with this, what if I could have or should have done something different, how can I live with this, how can I live without him, what if I could trade him for me?" It goes on and on.

Once we can realize that none of this, including the person's or animal's death, had anything to do with us, there is a clearing. Again, I believe our death date, time, and way, are set before we take on our body and our life here on planet Earth. This has been shown to me over and over. So, it is a gift, like being at the birth of anything, to be witness to such a miracle.

The moment of birth, the coming from somewhere on TO Earth and the moment of birth (what we call death) AWAY from Earth either back to or on to somewhere else. When I finally could receive this piece about death, I felt honored to have been gifted to have the premonitions of it for my dad, and to have been there in his last moments before leaving his body, and the moments to see only his body without him.

Offering:

If possible, open in any way that you can to the miracle of death. Understand that we are just leaving the body temple and we are still we, me. If we can, through the pain of loss, even with animals, know that they are still with us and have just shed their bodies, the ones that we have become accus-tomed to, but that they are still with us and more free.

Then, maybe, we can feel blessed to be witness and even a big part of birthing them to their next realm, where they will have their next adventures, experiences, learnings, loving that they will share with us when we, too, cross our rainbow bridges and are birthed into our other and next adventure.

TRAVELS OF THE MIND
AND SOUL

Many years after my father died, when I was in my twenties, I went to work in the computer business and worked in a little computer store in Princeton.

I fell in love with a man, Richard, who worked there – he was a Gentle Spirit. I just felt drawn to him in so many ways. At these moments we were just friends and later we would find a bigger story that was quite tragic. However, in these small moments of bliss I enjoyed the heightened sense of someone who seemed to really see the light around me.

One day Richard told me he would like to take me for a ride in his car and that it was a bit of an unusual car, but it was a car he loved. The day arrived and on a lunch break from our work we were going to go for a short ride in the car.

I approached the car and saw that it was my father's car, the car my father had when he died, the car that I rode in with him; a little white Renault with red seats. It was the only one of its kind for miles and I knew my mother had sold it to someone who lived not far from where I was now working.

As I remember, I was stunned, happy and crying, as if my dad were right there offering me the seat he always had for us to adventure on an amazing ride. My mother rode in the car maybe once, as she was totally against little cars, and my father buying and owning this car.

I sat down in the passenger seat. It smelled like my dad. How could this be? I started asking billions of questions, "How did you get this car?" "What made you buy it??" and on and on.

This wondrous man answered all of my questions and when I stopped talking and took it all in, Richard said, "Maybe your dad has given me his car, and now you, to care for."

Blessing:

This was a crazy experience as it was of my doing, my creating and my focus and directing behind it. Unlike many of the things I have witnessed, I was there FOR this one, I designed and made it happen, with help.

I felt a bit afraid and in wonder of my power in this, after my experience, as if I really had no idea who I was or what I truly had the power to do. So, this story for me is an incredible one in that how 'easy' it was to have the experience, to create the experience, and that with ease I direct and flow my energy in such a way.

It really made me 'sit up' and understand and look at how I was using my power and energy in all ways and other ways. Was I truly using all of my power for 'good'? Meaning, if I was disconnected from it or unconscious that when I spoke a negative thing about someone or something, I was adding negativity to them and towards them, so truly I was cursing them, without being really aware that I was doing this.

So I decided to, as much as I could and can, stay conscious of how I use my power, really focusing on using it for 'good.' If I am complaining, I stop that and draw that energy back and use it for a blessing. And if I don't catch it when I am doing it, then when I find it, I really focus on unwinding the energy that I focused unconsciously. I rework it into something I enjoy, and again, that is love and a blessing from me as much as I can do this, being human.

This I find makes me feel clear so I can hear the Divine speaking and or directing me (and receiving, too) and it makes me very happy.

Offering:

Become aware of your power as much as you are able. Use your power for good, blessings and love, instead of curses and harshness. We are here to write a bigger story on our Souls for love and compassion. Do that no matter what it looks like or what you think. Always do the loving thing. You have no idea and may not until you die, the gifts and love you are giving unknowingly.

WE

I have a dear friend, Sheila, who often travels with me.

At some moment we were setting up our moments that I was going to take her on another adventure. We were on the phone as I was leaving and I said to her, "We'll be there shortly, I'm running a little bit late."

When I showed up at Sheila's house, she seemed to be looking around my car as if she were looking for something.

I looked at her and she said, "You said, 'we are on our way,' so do you have Buddy (my dog), or someone else with you?"

I smiled and said, "It's just me and my Ten-Thousand Angels... So it's always we!"

WE ...*as Sheila remembers it*

I have been lucky enough to travel with Karen many times. The joke was always: "My husband and/or Buddy can't go this time. Would you like to have an adventure with me?" I always jumped at the chance because it was, indeed, always an adventure.

On one such occasion I got a call from Karen telling me she was running a little late and would text when she left her home. She lived about a half hour from me. A short time later, I got the text: "We are on our way."

'We? Hmmm. Wonder what I missed. Is she bringing her son, Conner? Maybe Buddy?' I'd have to wait and see. Meanwhile, I went about finishing getting my things together, all the while wondering who was adventuring with us.

When she arrived, I must admit I was curiously examining her car. I couldn't see a single soul. "Is it just you? Don't you have anyone with you?" "Just me," she replied. "Well, you said, 'We are on our way.' She laughed her infectious, sparkly laugh. She hadn't realized she had said that. Then the explanation, "I always travel with Ten-Thousand Angels. So, it is always We."

Blessing:

It is always such a comfort to ask to travel with Angels, to ask for Angels to help with everything – and to always ask to travel with Ten-Thousand Angels is such a happiness for me. A freedom and a knowing that I am so deeply cared for, blessed, cherished and loved.

Offering:

How would it be for you to ask for the Angels' help in everything or in one thing that you do. Ask for MORE than you need. Ask for more Angels in any and all situations that you can think of and see how it makes you feel. Blessed.

A SHARED PAST LIFE

After a long and tortured in-and-out relationship with Richard, years passed and I had not seen him in a very long time.

When I was in Chiropractic school I experienced a past life regression. I had had one before and was working with self-hypnosis, as I had been taking a class to become certified as a hypnotherapist.

I was working on the possibility of a past life that was causing me problems with being heavier than I wanted to be. This was my focus, but instead, as I started getting glimpses of a past life in which I was starving, it switched very dramatically to a life that looked very Victorian.

In this past life I saw myself married to the person that in this lifetime I knew as Richard. In that lifetime his name was Robert and my name was Katherine. We lived in a beautiful place and were very happy and affluent. My love for him was so deep. I recognized it immediately as the joy and soul connectedness that I had recognized and felt in this lifetime for him.

It was clear that in this lifetime we were young and I was ill. We were very much in love. I saw myself in a bed in a brightly-lit room with furnishings that looked like they came out of the movie 'A Christmas Carol.' I was sick, dying, and he and I both knew it. Nothing was going to save me from this lung disease – consumption?

My Robert was trying to look positive for me but I knew his heart. Soon, in this past life regression, I was in the death process and it was as if I were drowning. It was beautiful and light, as if there were water all around me. I was being pulled down deeper and deeper, it was this beautiful color of light blue and everything around me seemed perfect, except for the fact that I was dying.

I did not want to leave my beloved husband Robert. I kept calling to him and clinging to him. I remember asking him to promise me that he would find me, find me, no matter where I was. I grabbed his hands, then as he promised me he would look for me everywhere, I couldn't hold on to his hands any longer and was pulled underneath. It felt like I was drowning, but then a release of my body and then peaceful, loving, pain-free, easy, and beautiful. But I was angry because I did not want to be dead. I felt we had been cheated.

In the next scene I saw myself up in a tree, a spirit, a beautiful, beautiful tree, in a place I recognized completely as our tree, our meadow, our place. There sat Richard, now Robert, with my journal, sitting under the tree. I called to him and tried to wave the leaves and let him know I was right over his shoulder. I was right above him and he didn't even know it. He was crying and crying with my journal, leaning up against the tree with me right over the top of him. I could do nothing. I couldn't make him feel me, sense me, or see me.

I remember him opening my journal and seeing my pressed violets fall out. Then the past life ended and I woke. I could hardly breathe. I was so shocked at what I had found out about him and me, and how it was more real than anything I could have known. I kept this experience in my heart and on paper, which I carried around with me for many years.

Now several years later, both of us married with children, I met with him to catch up as old friends, old lovers. He always took my breath away.

I told him, "Wait," as he sat in front of me. "I have something I want to share with you. I wrote this down for you years ago when I had the experience." I handed him the paper on which I had written our story. It began: 'In this lifetime, your name was Robert, and mine was Katherine.'

He read only the first line, no more, and put the paper down and turned white. 'What?' I thought, 'He's not going to read the whole thing?'

Once he was ready to speak, he said, "Robert has always been a name that has been important to me. Enough so, that when my brother was born I insisted as a child that his name should be Robert. My parents appeased me because I caused such an issue with it, that his middle name is Robert. And Katherine; I insisted to my wife that if we had a girl she was to name her no other name... I would consider no other name... She had to be Katherine."

Blessing:

Surprising and eye-opening, somehow I expected that this dear man in my life would be touched by my past life memory of us and have some shadowing of it. But I had no idea he would 'know' its hangover into this lifetime as he did from his childhood, and for a whole lifetime in this life.

So to really understand as we reminisce with someone who has had a shared experience with us in this lifetime that others can be as fresh and available, was stunning to me. And the first of many adventures like this I would encounter into my future for myself and others. So much so that it became common, and even the first go-to place when someone was having any type of story, good or bad in this lifetime, was to look at the links to past lives and past lives between all who were involved in whatever the story – to see where their healing, behavior was coming from.

WHAT agreements did they have from the last lifetime into this one and what and where were they blocked, locked, or running free. This idea that Earth is a cruise, a theatre, where Souls come to learn and experience any story that we wish to expand the love in our Soul, frees us to take a bigger look at the deeper thing, behind the thing.

So this story continues to be a cornerstone in the deepness of what we don't know that drives us, and how we often just take it for granted and never wonder why. Hmmm.. Why does the name Robert mean so much to me (years and years and years before we had ever met)? No Grand Design? I don't think so. Not for one moment.

Offering:

You might feel driven by passions or hobbies or names, places, beliefs, that seem to come from who-knows-where. Often they are windows and doors into our past lives, and things we are carrying from that lifetime will offer us gifts in this lifetime. Crazy as all of this sounds, when you take a peek at all those who have gone before me have researched and experienced, you will find that it is a part of us. Who we have been in other times and places to experience as acting as a character in a theatre piece, we are still us having this experience in another time, place, and sometimes a different sex and even species. So, just be open and honor all that you have been, beyond this current incarnation.

DOGS TALKING

I was running errands in the closest 'big' town, about an hour away from where I live. Rushing a bit, my next stop was the local big box office store.

I felt a strange urge to park in an area where I had never parked before and I was a bit distracted because I had only a certain amount of time to do whatever I needed to do. So I just smiled at my Angels and said, "Okay!"

Up near the front I parked and gathered my list and stuff for whatever it was I was needing to buy. I slid out of the front seat of my truck to see a dog with its head out the back window of the vehicle next to me. I smiled and acknowledged the dog, as it was only a few feet away from me, with a nod.

The dog locked its eyes on me and I heard, as if someone was talking directly to me, 'I know you can hear me.' This dog was intense, not taking her eyes off me until after she had communicated this message. I could hear her, as I have 'talked' with animals before, but this was the first time one had reached out to me in this way where she sensed that I could understand her. I was stunned.

I communicated back to her as they speak, in a telepathic

language, 'Yes, I can hear you.'

Then, she started, 'You have to communicate a message to my owners. I'm very worried.'

Now, my mind is reeling. I say to her, 'I would be glad to communicate a message to your owners, but I don't know them.'

'Promise me you will tell them.'

'Okay, I will do my best, but I don't know them.'

Just about this time a very lovely woman, a bit older than myself I guessed, smiling, acknowledged me as I was looking at her dog as she got into the driver's seat. I imagined she was wondering why this woman was just standing there, maybe she was thinking, 'Well I guess my dog IS really cute.'

She got in the car and spoke to all of her dogs. (There were two other dogs in the SUV who were not talking to me. They just seemed to be standing witness, being partners, but not the leader in this idea to get someone to communicate to their owners.) She put her car in gear and started to pull out of the parking space. A bit panicked, the dog then said, 'You promised me you would talk to my owners! You Promised me!!!' Again stunned, I said, 'Yes, I will, but I don't know how I will do this as I don't know them...' The woman drove away and the dog, louder than ever, kept saying, 'You promised me.'

So, I become a crazy person. I jump back in my truck and intend to follow this woman in her SUV as the dog is still looking at me out the window. They are a few cars ahead of me and they catch the light where I don't, so they disappear, even though I turn in the same direction they have turned.

I'm looking everywhere for them to see if I can find any way to talk to her at her next stop.

Now I know that I'm completely nuts, thinking, what would it be like, from her point of view, if someone followed me away from the store – a little scary. However, the dog keeps talking to me and I keep trying to negotiate, telling the dog I have no way to find the owner, no way, no possibility of keeping my promise to her...

The dog then tells me they can be found on the internet – her owner can be found on the internet. Now I think I've really lost my mind, as this was a number of years ago when the internet was not as popular as it is now.

The only thing I can remember is the word 'Granite' on a sign on the side of the car. So I make a deal with the dog that if I can find her owner on the internet, like she was telling me through sending images, I will contact her and let her know whatever it is that she wishes to tell her.

Again, now I really think I'm nuts. I drive for an hour to an office we had in our local town to get on the internet and see if I can find anything that would let me know that I was, or was not, crazy in one way or another.

Now one hour later, without any of the supplies that I needed from the office supply store, I arrive at the office with the internet access. I get on the internet and with much, much internal nay-saying, I feel myself doing my duty to type in the word 'granite,' knowing I would not find anything, that the experience would be over, and I could telepathically send to the dog the message that I could not find her owner, and that would be that.

However, I type in the search for 'granite,' hit the enter button, and the first thing that comes up is a picture of this woman, her three dogs, her husband, the business they own, and all the information on how to contact them. I feel the dog smiling in front of me as if to say, 'I told you so.'

Now I'm committed, feeling even crazier than before. I decided to not call this woman, but to send her an email through her business address. The email, as I recall, went something like this:

'Greetings, my name is Dr. Karen. I am the person that you saw standing next to your dog and car in the parking lot, at the shopping center. Your dog spoke to me, and wants to give you a message. She has not told me what that message is yet. I know this sounds so crazy. If you wish you can contact me at...'

Wow, I just kept thinking, 'How unbelievable is all of this?!'

So, the owner did respond to me! She left a voicemail saying she would love to talk to me, that they had used communicators before with the dogs, and she would love for me to talk to all of the dogs.

We made an appointment for me to come to their home, where Millie, the dog who said 'I know you can hear me,' would talk about how deeply worried she was about the owners, especially the husband; that he seemed very sad and upset, especially after he was on the phone (the dog said all of this). The owner smiled a sad smile and said that yes, in fact, the husband's mom had been very ill and he had been on the phone a lot, as she lived in another part of the country. They had been getting frequent updates about her health as she had been in and out of the hospital. So, Millie the dog had cause to really worry because the whole family was very different with what was happening. Even though nothing in her day-to-day life had changed, she really had no other options than to communicate though me, what she was seeing happen with her guardians.

I spoke with the other dogs also, one who told me she had been locked in a closet in her previous home, and was terrified of the dark. The current owner said this was probably the case, as she had been removed from her previous home and was a rescue.

I recommended some Bach Flower rescue remedy for her, and we worked on some other personal things she wished to share. The other dog didn't speak much to me, she just wanted to let her owners know how much she loved and appreciated them and what they did for her (all the dogs were rescued), and that she too had been concerned and loved her life with them.

Dusty, the owner, and I became friends and years later I would be a constant fixture on her radio show, where at some moment we would share how we met though her beloved dog Millie, who talked to me.

– from Dusty, the owner

(Please note, some details differ, but we have included them exactly as each person recalled.)

Several years back, while at our granite shop business, our office manager came and told me I had a call from a woman who said, "I know this may sound kind of strange, but there was a lady driving a gold Jeep that had a Granite sticker on the windows. I saw her yesterday in the Staples parking lot and she had three dogs with her. Is she there, and is it possible to speak with her?"

Tina and I both raised our eyebrows, looking perplexed, but I took the call.

The lady on the phone said, "You don't know me. My name is Dr. Karen. I was parked next to your SUV yesterday in front of Staples. We smiled as you were backing out."

She then said, "One of your dogs, the black and white Border Collie-looking dog, caught my eye and said, 'I know you can understand me. I need to tell my mom that I am worried about her mother who just visited.' Your dog was very concerned and since she reached out to me I felt compelled to contact you."

Well, it wasn't actually my mother who had recently visited, it was my mother-in-law from down in the Valley/Phoenix.

Dr. Karen and I had a very nice conversation which I thoroughly enjoyed – we just connected. I mentioned it to my husband that night and we were both perplexed as to what Millie was trying to tell us.

A few days later my mother-in-law was admitted to the hospital and had a pacemaker put in her chest. We didn't know she was having heart challenges since we didn't talk with her daily. However, we were ever so grateful to know that it was caught in time and taken care of.

I contacted Dr. Karen, let her know, and thanked her for reaching out to me, telling her what had transpired. I invited her over to the house to meet her in person and to meet Millie, as well as our other two girls, Maggie and Mollie.

It was an instant connection, meeting Dr. Karen. We both are avid animal lovers, spiritual, intuitives... Although I am not as honed with my gift as she.

As we were visiting, she asked me, "Do you know you have a spirit in your house?" I just smiled and asked what it was she was picking up on.

Dr. Karen stated there is an elderly woman named Anna who had befriended our 'three girls.' She had lived on the site where our house was, back in the 1800s. She was a loner, never married, kind of ostracized from society and she had not ever cared for animals. However, she was getting to know our girls and really enjoyed their company. She asked me (through Karen) if it was okay for her to stay and be friends with our girls.

And I said, "Yes, of course!"

I knew we had a spirit in our house due to a few prior circumstances... I had sensed her, actually smelled her, mostly in the doorway to my office as I would walk in and out.

There was an instance one day where I heard a loud sound in the living room. To give you a visual, we had three ledges staggered above our fireplace. On each ledge, I had three to five crosses we had collected over the years, standing up, on top of each other, layered/staggered themselves. A two-foot plain wooden cross that had been behind two other crosses, closest to the wall, had fallen onto our hardwood floor and the other two crosses were still standing in their upright, layered positions on the ledge.

I was quite puzzled, but put it back up on the ledge, behind the two other crosses and went about my day.

That evening I explained the happening to my husband. He said, "Interesting. That cross was from my first wife." I didn't even know that! We had collected so many crosses throughout our many travels over the years it was hard to remember all of them and where they came from, so I just figured it was one of ours. We then laughed about it, saying, "Well, I guess our 'Anna' didn't like having it here!" So, I took it down and replaced it with another, and donated that one ;-)

Periodically I would say to our 'girls,' "Where's Anna?" and they would start looking around. It made me feel so good knowing she was there and watching over them.

When we moved four years ago, I 'talked' with Anna and invited her to come along with us to our new home. We had lost two of our girls at that point, only having Millie left when we moved into our new home. Anna never joined us though. She stayed with the home on Pleasant Street.

When we got new tenants to rent the house, I asked them if they believed in spirits and if they were afraid of them. Finding out they were okay with them, I told them about Anna. For the first year or so they had quite a few encounters with Anna, all in a fun way.

I am grateful for my encounter with Dr. Karen and the friendship we have still maintained all these years, all because of our sweet Millie Vanilly communicating with her that one day years ago, looking through the Jeep window, meeting her eyes and 'talking' with her.

Blessing:

I am still in wonder, even after all these years, as to this lovely dog being so passionate about getting a communication to her guardians. She has caused me to stop, wait, listen, and communicate back a lot more than I would have if I had not had this experience. Again, this didn't at the time seem like it was going to be a gift (another blessing from this story) as it seemed full of problems to overcome. (The best lessons often are this way!) So, these God-filled, Dog-filled moments have continued to bless me for a lifetime.

Offering:

Where can you listen, stop, learn and return a message to an animal that you meet? Many are willing to share conversations and concerns with us humans, and if you receive a message I would encourage you to be brave and share it, as it might change everything for the animals and humans involved.

SPECIAL 'TALENT'

After my father's death I spent a lot of time trying to get rid of whatever my special 'Talent' was. At some moment I even signed up for a channeling class taught by an older German woman, who was very matter-of-fact about channelling Spirit Guides and such. I loved her in her way of being. Emotionally, she was about the Spirit world the same as she would have been to teach you to cook.

I was one of about twenty-eight students. We were to share why we had come to learn channeling in her class. I was about the last to speak and I said, "If you know how to turn this on in someone, I am SURE you know how to turn it off."

She made a very big show of emotion to the fact that I should not wish to give this 'Talent' away, and said that I should go about developing it more. With this in mind, it wasn't surprising that there were a few things I hadn't noticed about this 'Talent' as time passed, as I kept trying to ignore it as well as all my other 'Talents,' just to be normal.

This 'Talent' of having a deep understanding of when someone might die seems indeed to be a talent. I would not understand my unique connection to it until many years had passed.

Besides the huge impact of the directness of my knowing about my father's death and knowing how it came to pass, I started understanding a very odd thing that would happen to me before someone would die, whether human or an animal. I've had this happen a number of times but never recognized it as a truth until this moment happened in my life.

I live in a very rural area of Arizona. Folks live here, many off-the-grid like myself, with many stories. People seem to help out all they can whenever they can. It seems a place stuck in a time long ago when folks would offer a helping hand.

One eve, my then husband, my kids and I were driving in our tiny truck back to the ranch where we lived. A handful of teenagers were hitching a ride back to the ranch, to the home of one of the children's grandparents. We had no room in the front, as there were four of us squashed in the cab, so they jumped in the bed of the truck. There were five of them, laughing and messing around, happy for the ride home so they wouldn't have to walk another eight or so miles.

I, being the mom-type, kept cautioning them, "Sit down in the bed kids! We don't want any of you to fall out!!"

They laughed. I was serious. All the while I saw four of the children very distinctly, in the early evening sunlight they sparkled, it seemed. The colors on their clothes bright, they were all bright except for the biggest boy. It was his grandparents' where we were to deliver them. He was a beautiful light brown, heavy-set boy; again, the biggest of the group. He was gentle and sweet, soft-spoken. All of this and I could not 'see' him. He was as if in a mist; there, but not there.

I believe I even made a comment to my family, something to the effect; "Do you see that kid?" So, the whole ride I kept looking at him, trying to understand if it was where he was sitting, the light, my eyes, the colors of he and his clothing.

Then it was time to drop them off at the end of the long driveway to his grandparents' home. They all jumped out and thanked us, and as the five walked up the driveway, I was smiling inside at how polite they all were for kids their age, and then it happened again.

All walking more or less in a row, I saw all of their backs, but his... Well... I saw him, but I didn't... It's hard to describe. Maybe as if he were disappearing – misty; there but not there. He spoke to me. He was real and there, but to me, I could not 'see' him the same as the others, and also strange was the fact that I could not describe him. I could not tell you the details of him. I could not tell you all of the expressions on his face or the details of the color of his clothing. So weird.

Even when I got home, I tried to describe him and asked my family what he looked like, as I felt I had a drawing within my heart of the faces and clothing of the other four, but with him I could not get it. My family thought this was odd as they noticed no difference and thought, 'Okay Mom's just being Mom; we'll play along,' and so they described him to me as best they could, but they really hadn't noticed as I had, anything except a few details about him.

I was haunted by this as I had seen many, many, many odd things before: past lives in people, aura colors, what looked like smoke coming from a painful body part, to name a few, but I had never been unable to see someone who WAS there. As the evening wore on I put it out of my mind, realizing that maybe it was something I would not understand. I had had this happen in the past as well. I let it go, and tried to not think about it any more as it seemed disturbing.

The next day came and went with school for the kids, and work, and life. When we all made it back home and dinner was happening, homework in the making, my then husband said, "Did you hear about the accident?"

"No," I said, "what accident?"

"Those kids we picked up yesterday, they were hitching a ride back in to town. When the vehicle they were in turned into the highway, they were hit by a truck. All of the kids were taken to the hospital, all are going to be okay except the big black kid. He was killed."

I was beyond speechless. Had my Angel been showing me again, foretelling a death that I could do nothing about? As my father's and others? That I now was pondering deep and hard. This was awful! I was upset with God. Why could I not have kept him safe? Especially when I felt such a huge need to lecture them about being safe by sitting in the bed of the truck.

Then a Grace came to me, "Our time is our time," locked in time designed by us and God. You cannot change it or move it. It is the Plan. "Your own unique way and time," is what I deeply understood. Somehow in that moment I felt honored that I had been foretold, that he was already leaving, even as we picked him up. His Spirit was only a mist, already on his path to leaving his body.

After this recognition I had many of these moments, one of them with a very famous horse. Again, after I had given him his treatment and even during his treatment, I couldn't see him. This was dramatic enough for me that my current husband watched me go back and talk to this horse, negotiating with him; telling him that I hoped that I would see him again, and not to do this, not to leave us, and that this information that I had about him (not being able to 'see' him), that I was really hoping that it would not be true, that I would see him again after his arrival in Florida.

He looked at me as though things were set in stone and as though both of us knew we would never see each other again. I cried and rubbed on him so much. Within about two weeks he had died in a tragic way.

This also happened with a man who is a hero to all of us, as he was a firefighter and a Hotshot. I saw him sitting in his living room on the sofa as I was giving his wife and mother-in-law their treatments. He sat there and I could not quite see him. As I was giving the family treatments and I knew he had been having some shoulder pain, I, as usual, just brushed it off as a funny thing. I knew his fire fighting season was about to start and so I thought, 'I'm not seeing him because I won't see him for months, he probably won't be home when I am home.'

This, however, was an omen that would later comfort his wife, as the horse story would many months later comfort his owner. This man and his team would become known around the world for their deaths and the sacrifices they made. He and his team would all die together, and again, somehow for me it is a Grace and blessing of knowing, and a gift when told to the living, that the path was set, and there was not any earthly thing that could have changed it.

Blessing:

Even though these didn't look like blessings at the time I took them very much to be in the end as what a blessing for me to understand the gift here. So many things we believe about death, so many are just not true, and what a gift to know that nothing could be done. What a gift to know it is part of a bigger thing, a story that we are witness, partner, parent to. That when we look deeply we will find the gifts in these stories that our beloved ones, human and animal, agreed to give us. In this way for me it was fantastic!

I bow my head again to be in wonder and awe of the Great Plan, Design and Love that allows us to explore and experience these Soul stories with one another. Remarkable!

Offering:

In these stories I offer that maybe to look at death and dying in another way might free you and help you to find a peace that you might not have experienced yet around a Soul's leaving their body temple. May I offer these were deep gifts given to me across all beliefs that I had been taught. Yet upon reflection, I believe they are embedded in everything I was taught, but did not understand in the way I do now.

We are all pieces of the Divine. Ebbing and flowing from this amazing Divine place. Individual and yet part of the

ONE, we journey to earth to learn and grow and love. To love, love, love and to touch and hold. Then we return to ONE to share and interpret our experiences once again though a love so great I believe we cannot even imagine it.

And so we all flow. Everything, all kisses of the Divine, brief and beautiful, full of wonder. We all have our determined expiration date. It might be the moment or before we arrive, to a very old and long life. Chosen, it is all chosen, and we will return to each other's arms, hearts, hooves, etc. To love even more deeply and fully with the experiences each has written on our Souls by ourselves and by each other. How glorious!

CONNER

When my son, Conner, was just a few months old, we went to visit some Buddhist monks who were spending some time in Flagstaff doing some traditional Buddhist ceremonies in a church there.

It was a chilly evening and I remember being haunted by going to this event, thinking somehow that Conner was so special that he would be taken from me by this group of Buddhist monks; that somehow they would recognize him to be a Soul that they had traveled with in the past. I talked to myself about how crazy this was and tried to convince myself that I was probably hormonal or something.

When we entered the church, the young and older monks were milling around quietly greeting everyone. Some were thoughtfully preparing for the ceremony that would take place once everyone was gathered. I felt this setting was a very peaceful and loving environment and relaxed and got in line with Conner in my arms to be given a beautiful golden yellow prayer string which they placed around their and our necks.

The room became more and more hushed as the time was coming to do the ceremony. I was hanging back a bit, waiting to sit down as Conner could be squirmy. I was hoping to get the most out of having to sit and be quiet.

Just before we sat down in a quieted room as folks were finding their seats, a young Buddhist monk came over to me as if he were going to speak to me, or perhaps ask something of me. I tilted towards him, Conner in my arms. He made no contact with me. He spoke only to Conner (and to no other person in the room at the event for that matter).

The monk looked at Conner very intently, bowed his head, then looked up again, touched his golden prayer tie, looked him in the eye and said, "I will pray for you, every day for the rest of my life," and then he walked away.

Truly, for the rest of the event I held my breath, considering even more deeply than before, 'who was this child?'

Blessing:

I learned again how much wonder there is in the world and how we must listen to our intuition, that often shows up in feelings in our guts and stomach and around our hearts and chests. I also learned about choice; that we have Divine appointments that we all will show up for, and we always have a choice. My worries were blessed by this young monk who acknowledged something in Conner and I was elevated to the highest level of experience with it, because I stayed open and willing to receive no matter what it was going to look like.

Offering:

Be open and honoring of what the Great One is offering

you and wants to give you, and always know you have a choice. That said, no matter how crazy, scary, etc., what the Great One is giving is ALWAYS beyond your wildest dreams and so beautiful for you, even if in the moment it doesn't seem that way. Trust and jump!

GRANDMOTHER SPIDER

I was on a visit to the Hopi reservation. We had just returned a Hopi elder that I knew back to his home. He had spent time with some of my friends from Italy and me in order to share teachings and stories with us on my land, which has a petroglyph site on it. Now, my friends and I were relaxing, shopping in an open market of Hopi artisans after our beautiful time with him.

As we quietly took in the lovely items these people had crafted, I started a conversation with one of the Native women. Even though I am not Native, I have been taught by different Native people and teachers from different tribes and was adopted into a Native family many years ago. I was strongly drawn to this woman and in my Native teachings I knew that this woman was holding a gift for me, a teaching that Great One wanted me to learn. So, now I will share it with you.

We started speaking about spiders, as there was a piece of jewelry that had a spider on it. I told her how I love spiders. My friends made faces and said how much they didn't like spiders. This woman smiled and looked me in the eye and started sharing the story.

She said, "I have a teenage daughter, and my daughter has

become where she doesn't want me to know as much about her as I did when she was little. She is growing up; she will say nothing to me. Day after day I would talk to her and say things like, 'How is school going? Still having trouble in that math class? You had a fight with your best friend? How are things now? Please don't allow your boyfriend to talk to you badly, so that you feel unhappy with yourself...'

"Days passed like this where she would come home and stay in her room, talk on the phone, and most of the time when she was home, she was in her room not speaking much to me, if at all. Every day I would ask one question or two, but they would be questions that I knew of things that were happening in her life.

"Finally, she asked in a bit of an angry way, 'How do you know these things? How could you know to ask these questions?'

"I smiled and I said, 'Grandmother Spider of course.'"

She said her daughter was quiet and frowned. She said to her daughter, "When I go in to clean your room, I talk to Grandmother Spider who lives near your window. I ask her how you are doing. She tells me everything that is happening with you because she sees, hears and knows all of it, as she lives with you in your room."

This Native woman smiled at me even bigger than before and nodded her head, a thank you to Grandmother Spider, as her daughter started to share everything with her after she found out how much her Grandmother Spider and her mom cared about her.

Blessing:

My heart opened so much with this experience, as I love insects, critters and creatures of all types. I have always tried to honor their lives, even the ones we find difficult such as flies and mosquitoes.

I've had brushes in the past when I had been talked to, taught by them, and this experience opened even more to ongoing conversations and wisdom and being even more deeply in service to those who live with and near us.

These teachings have always been deep and full of wonder, especially from a perspective that is so different and often much wiser than our own. So, I am in love with all of the creatures that live with me, work with me, near me, and who teach me things I would have never known.

Yes, with much honor and deep gratitude to those creatures we usually kill, hate, are afraid of, try to exterminate; I am grateful for all that you have taught me and how patient you have been in the teaching of me.

Offering:

Animals or creatures that you might hate, or be afraid of, ones that you might kill; take a moment to be quiet within yourself and ask them to talk to you. Ask them a question or to share with you about their lives. In your house for example, what do they know or see? You might reconsider killing them, relocate them, or ask them how you might be able to help them. You might be deeply surprised, deeply, and pleasantly, surprised.

PROJECTING

There was a moment in my life when I was dating a man who I felt was incredibly vast. At the same time I had been studying to try to understand my strange psychic or other abilities. In this quest I had a number of teachers and my abilities always seemed to be beyond theirs. They could train me only for short periods of time before I seemed to outgrow them – quickly. This sometimes caused jealousy on my teacher's part, or a sense of not really knowing how to direct me next.

I was in the stage where I was just ending with the teacher and decided to play some games with this Dear One in my life. He was always up for these things and would always one-up me in some funny, crazy way. My challenge to myself was to sit in meditation (I had not told him I was going to try this) and see if I could enter his body and see what he was doing. (Of course I asked spiritual permission first!)

Slowly, I sank into my meditative place. Darkness, deep darkness. Then I felt warm water on my hands. However, when I opened my 'eyes' they were not my hands. They were giant hands, and I was looking down from a much higher place at a very different angle from how I usually viewed the world. I viewed my giant hands in a white sink; they were moving under the warm running water and somehow it all seemed very common, like nothing at all was out of place. I was shocked. What had I done? I was very disoriented.

Then, I realized I had been granted access inside my boyfriend's body and that he was standing at his kitchen sink washing dishes. I had access to stand within him (he not being aware, but again, I had asked permission to do this and had gotten it) and completely experience what every aspect of his body was doing, without having any power to change anything he was doing. I was a complete passenger, being able to feel, smell, see what he was doing.

I had a heightened sense of awareness, like how tall he was. I was shocked at how everything looked from up so high. Also, how it felt to have such large hands that seemed a chore to move about, where my own hands (I didn't know until this moment) were much more delicate and easier to move in finer ways. I was even aware of the muscles in his/my arms and how they felt and were moving to grasp the dish and sponge to clean it and the way his/my hand closed and how the movement seemed so very awkward.

Then there was the feeling of walking. I felt like a Franken-stein. It seemed he was bulky with teetering movements as he/I covered a huge amount of space in just one step, as he/I moved away from the sink to the dining area when the few dishes he/I were washing were clean.

I don't know how long this mediation lasted; not very long, only moments I believe, but it would change me forever. I popped out of his body and saw him in the dining room, looking at something on the table, now I was on the outside of his body. I observed this very 'normal,' regular moment. I was shocked and surprised at how intense all of this had felt to me, both on his insides and now on the outside. All of my senses seemed intensified a hundred-fold.

The moment I 'thought' this thought I was back in my room, my body. Again, I felt a bit shocked as if I had been placed or replaced back in my body, still with all of the awareness of his body and how that felt. Maybe this is like getting in and out of different cars and driving them; how different each one is and how you remember the feeling each one gives you as you drive it. This experience was a bit like this idea, but much more intense and full of sensation. I believe the next thing was to go to work, and so I did and later called my boyfriend.

When I did the meditation I had made note of the time. I called him and asked if he knew what he was doing at the time I had this experience. He said he really couldn't remember, but that he had been home for the day. I asked, "Did you do dishes today?" and before he answered I described to him the few dishes he did, in which way he did them, how he reached from the one counter to wash them and how he had placed them in a towel on the counter top, and in which order. I described what the light in the room looked like.

He was quiet and said yes, he had done this and in that exact way. He had forgotten. Who wouldn't, it was a mundane thing, why would he remember, we just try to get these things done, our minds on other things. But for me, it was life-changing, washing the dishes with him.

He asked "How did you know? Did you come and remotely view me?"

I said, "Well, yes and no. I asked permission of your Guardian Angel to enter your body and see what you were doing." I was granted permission and it was crazy how I could feel what your hands feel!! And how crazy it is to see the things you see from that high up! To feel your body and see why you chose to do the dishes in what order, and how beautiful the morning light was in the kitchen and how it seemed you noticed that for a moment. Then, when you were done, you walked over to the dining room and to the table. I felt you walking and how giant you feel. Then I popped out of your body just as you were reaching for some mail and watched you from the outside for a moment. Then I was back in my body; back here."

He was quiet for a bit. I sensed he was reviewing these moments in his mind. Then he said, "I didn't feel you inside of me, but I did sense something in the room watching me when I reached for the mail."

"That's right!" I said, "You turned and looked right at me! It was right after that, that I popped back into my own body. He laughed his hearty laugh and said, "So, I caught ya!" Then he asked something about could I do the dishes in the future without him being there, as that would be really helpful.

This same boyfriend and I would learn to play at many energetic things. We would send messages to each other throughout the day from our minds, what we might call telepathy. He, being more creative or humorous than I would do very funny things with the talents we were developing with each other.

My daughter and I were planning a long overdue adventure. We had been invited to travel to Vermont and Canada to help a friend and her daughter try to figure out where they wanted to move. It would be a road trip with the girls. My daughter was about four and my friend's daughter was a teenager.

Off from the East Coast we went, excited to be on the road, our lives in the rear view mirror for a week or more of fun.

Then I started seeing and hearing my boyfriend's name everywhere. And I mean everywhere. Billboards with his first name that seemed twenty feet tall. I saw eighteen-wheelers with his name at least six feet tall or taller, some in fluorescent colors. The announcer on the radio was saying his first name over and over.

At first I was shocked, as it seemed as if his name was being thrown at me; like it was hitting me physically, like someone would hit you unexpectedly with a baseball. Coincidence, I thought. Must be just a popular name the further north we go. Then it did 'hit' me. These big loud names seemed to be shouting themselves about every two hours. Yes! As I watched, it was every two hours, to the minute almost. 'Hmmm, are you sending me stuff?' I thought. No coincidence. (There are none anyway!)

Days later I was able to make a phone call to him. We said our greeting and cooing. Then I said, "I have been seeing your name and hearing it everywhere! It's so crazy! Like everywhere?! Especially every two hours. Are you sending me this?"

There was that silence and the smile I could see through the phone. Then he said, "Well, I didn't want you to forget about me."

I hurumphed, "How could I have forgotten about you!! Your name has been everywhere!"

Again, that silent smile, "Well, then it worked didn't it."

Blessing:

This experience taught me several powerful lessons. The first was with the slightest intention, and I do mean slightest, what I could accomplish. This was terrifying and incredibly freeing, all at the same moment.

How much power did I have that I was hiding or that I wasn't using? Or was I using it but in ways that maybe I didn't understand or connect to? Hmmm. This is something I still ponder and experiment with.

The next blessing was how deeply connected we really, really are. Again, maybe in ways that we are not consciously aware of, but how deep that tie is. So why wouldn't we be able to connect and know? There is so much 'old' knowledge and teaching around telepathy. It seems to me we are wired for it and it takes a lot more energy for us to turn it off and not pay attention to it than to be with it and know it is how we are designed. It is in our survival to 'know.'

I have often wondered, do we get sick because we feel we have to shut off our knowing? I know I suffered for many years knowing and wanting to be 'normal' and trying to not know all the time. Another gift was that it can be fun, play – this intangible tie we have to everything. I love that I can lovingly laugh at how we can use these talents.

Offering:

Today, how could you send a message or look at someone or something remotely? See if you can from a happy heart, send a loving message and then maybe follow up and see if it was received. You might be surprised at what you can do, that you didn't even know you were capable of, with just a little focused intention and some fairy dust.

HORSE TELEPATHY

A few years ago I was gifted the opportunity to work with famous horse trainers who basically ride and train horses with telepathy. I didn't know this at the time, however it had been a prayer of mine to the Great One, that if there was anyone else out there in the Universe who was playing around with telepathy and horses, I would meet them.

I had been doing some work with my own horses and calling them with my mind or talking to them with my mind with no external voices. I felt I had been doing quite well with these experiments and was doing all of this in secret, sharing it with no one but God. I wasn't sure if I was the only person on the planet who was actually playing around with this, or pondering this idea, or maybe even working on the next levels of these possibilities.

I arrived at the trainers' place with the new friend who had invited me, clueless. I had no idea what God had in mind for me, or the magnitude of what I was about to receive.

First was to be my evaluation to see where I was on my spectrum of ability for riding in their way. (Remember that I had no idea these folks rode and taught folks how to ride and train horses using telepathy yet.) My first clue was that

I was given instructions to ride the horse, from one of my teachers, with no foot, calf, leg, seat, or hands.

To those who ride horses, you understand I was being asked to ride this horse with no aids – none. To those of you who don't ride, the usual way we all are taught to ride horses, no matter what the discipline, is to use our bodies. We use isolated parts of our bodies which our horses are taught to understand and interpret as us 'asking/telling/even commanding' the horse to perform certain movements or behaviors, or gaits, or whatever we want them to do in any given moment.

Sometimes a whip or riding crop is also used to 'help,' to 'tell' the horse what we what him or her to do. Horsemanship and horseback riding, again, no matter the discipline, behaves as if the horse must be treated as a being who has to be shown through our body's movements, or the rope, or whip, or whatever pressure on them or some part of their body, how to behave with us. All of these I was uncomfortable with as my experience of them was so much bigger.

I would venture to say that we are the limited ones in how we view horses in this area, as almost every training and riding technique out there involves the horse's interpretation of our pressure on him. As we humans like to say, "the reward of the release of pressure."

But if you ask you will find many, if not all, aware and even some unaware horse folks, making note of the rider or owner thinking something and the horse just doing it immediately, often even before the thought was completed by the thinker. Many a horse, too, has been punished for this, as in the training world we have this idea that horses should not do what we have thought (telepathy) until we physically ask the horse. If they 'jump the gun' and answer our thought, not waiting for the proper ask in the physical, they are punished.

I think we are nuts! All animals 'speak' telepathically, or if we wish to say, intuitively. So, they get punished for the thing we ask with our minds that they answer and do, but we are mad because they didn't wait for our bodies to ask their bodies. Yet we also get upset if they are too slow in their response to us. Not an easy soul path these horses have chosen to travel with us crazy folks!

So, in this first encounter with this trainer, I was asked to ride with my mind, in so many words. Do remember I didn't know this was how they taught and rode, so I was a bit panicked and trying to understand by asking questions along the way.

It was crazy to start to think and feel in that moment for the first time I was on a horse who totally understood my thoughts. (Later, I would think how every horse understands my thoughts and how deeply sad it is that the majority of them have to not listen to us in this way because we are so reckless and untrained in how we use our thoughts and how and what we send out that they must try to read our craziness in other ways.)

This horse moved with my thoughts in such a clear way that I noticed my mind and thoughts became clearer. Do remember the trainer was right there next to me, protecting her horse from what I did or did not know or do. So in a metaphysical way she, as well as this advanced horse, helped me sort out my thoughts, get clear and precise, and line up everything in my body, soul and mind around this precise telepathic conversation I was sending and receiving with this horse.

I cannot even begin to tell you the feeling that I had from this first experience of being telepathically aware with a horse. It was every childhood belief, every dream I had about myself and horses, animals, unicorns, life. Everything I knew to be true in my heart but could not touch or had not touched in this way came true for me in this moment. All of this and more, and my secret, my longing, my little experience and experiments with my own herd had been blown from just the starting point to an Olympic level.

Now what? By the end of my first day in this magical place I realized they taught telepathy, had a deep and quiet loyalty to it, and their facility was devoted in every way to this teaching. They realized I had no idea this is what they did and asked how on earth I showed up there and even more, how was I accepted in without proper protocol? Well, I thought in a panic, it was a variety of God things, fairy dust and magic and I announced with great confidence, "I had the Mark Russell card."

The trainer who had been stern, now laughed out loud and said, "Okay..." with a big smile. My dear friend Mark knew these folks and had encouraged me to go on this adventure since I was given the chance. I would be given an assignment to do that evening to catch up to what the two other students already knew. My dear traveling friend, Sheila (who is my Ten-Thousand Angel friend), was watching the whole time. We both were left with a story we would both giggle about, and I would be in wonder of for many years to come.

As the week went on, there were more wonders in store

for me and I started to feel comfortable and believe that life with horses could be this way always. I was given four lessons a day while I was at this amazing facility. Two were riding and two were in-hand work, or working with the horse with me standing on the ground and no one riding him.

One of the days that I was doing in-hand work, I was given the privilege of working with the Master's personal horse. This was a stallion who is a Lusitano, very accomplished and very sensitive. I was excited and nervous as I felt that I was a preschooler at this school and at the skills I needed to work with telepathy with any horse, much less this one.

Out into the arena he came. Beautiful, majestic and noble, this Lusitano proudly took his place in the indoor arena. The indoor area was large enough for a trainer to be giving a lesson to a rider on a horse at one end and for another to be also training at the other end, or the entire space could also be used if needed for one horse and rider.

There was a beautiful and elegant seating area for people who wished to be viewing whatever was happening in the arena. I remember lots of eyes looking at me; especially at this stunning horse who had great presence.

I was with a very accomplished student of this telepathic work who was overseeing my in-hand work, and our teacher was with a rider at the other end of the arena, also watching. I was given the smallest task to ask this horse to travel in a circle around me; to bend his body in a precise way and for him to travel with me. Remember, I am learning with this amazing horse (they wanted me to feel a horse who could communicate at such a high level), sending the pictures from my mind. I had a small training whip to just ever-so-gently touch him if I or he was not quite getting it right.

So I started. It is going pretty well, I'm thinking, as I am a beginner and he is reading my thoughts so well. I feel again as though I am a preschooler, excited to be using the alphabet, exchanging my new skill with a being who can speak many languages, has written many books with my alphabet, and used it in ways I haven't even begun to dream.

At some moment this horse stops and turns and stares at me. Eyes full in me. He won't move, no matter what I send him, and no matter what I do with my gently tapping whip.

I turn to my advanced helper, again with all eyes on me including this stallion, and ask for help. I say to her, "I know I am doing something wrong but I can't figure out what it is."

She looked at me with her gentle, perfect German poise and posture and said, "You are not sending fast enough."

"What?" I said. "I don't understand."

She repeated and then added, "You are not sending fast enough. He is becoming frustrated with you because you are not sending him the pictures fast enough for him to do what he needs to know to do next. You are too slow, and he is letting you know."

I looked up and they all were still looking at me as if all of them, including this stallion, were seeing the lack in what I was sending from my mind, and all of them had taken as much as they could of it, and they were very glad the stallion finally said something.

I thought the stallion was smiling. I imagined he thought,

'Finally, she will realize that she is torturing me with her slow and non-crisp images. Thank goodness, now she will try to do better!'

So, I tried again. As if I weren't humble to begin with, I sure was even more humbled now. My feeling was that we both did better, he was more patient with me and I a bit faster and more precise. We did well and I was so grateful for his strength and wisdom. He was a strong soul who taught me well. He taught me to be clear, clearer, yet clearer still and concise, more concise, yet more concise still. I have thought of him and thanked him many times for this deep and powerful lesson and the deep gifts from this place, these people and their horses; that it is rarely ever as it seems.

Blessing:

I felt as if I had found my clan of folks who were trying and believed as I did and do about horses. I believe, as Mark Russell has expressed, that we know (and are operating) on only a fraction of what horses know and can do. For me, this and these experiences have given me even more courage, ideas and excitement to go forward with more telepathy experiments and incorporating this as a way of living.

Offering:

Envision another way of being with your animals (as well as trees and all life and presences on the planet). Play with experimenting with telepathy (sending pictures and emotions) to your beloved beings and any of the beings around you. Be open and see what happens.

THE DOG WHO SAID "I DON'T LIKE MY FOOD"

A few years ago I had the blessing to be offered to stay with a friend's friend who had a beautiful home in an area where I was working. I did not know this woman and was grateful that she would be so kind and generous to offer for me to stay with her in her home for about a week.

I showed up at her home in my rental car after flying in and she and her little dog greeted me at the door. She was elegant, as was her home, and almost immediately I was distracted by her lovely little dog wanting me to tell her that she, the dog, didn't like her new food.

Her owner was showing me all of the particulars of the home; the security code, who to watch out for if I came in late, which cats and dogs would try to sneak in or out, how the different guest bedrooms had different themes, which of my friends had stayed in which rooms, and how she chose this room for me after considering and consulting with one of the friends who stayed with her often. Meanwhile, I was only partly paying attention because this woman's dog kept looking up at me and telling me about the new food.

We finally made our way into this woman's lovely, spacious

kitchen. The dog hadn't taken her eyes off me since I had stepped through the door. She had followed us everywhere, continuing to look up at me, saying, 'I don't like my new food,' over and over and over.

When there was a short pause in the conversation, I asked if this woman had changed her dog's food recently. The woman tipped her head as if the question was totally out of context. I am sure it was for her, but for me this was all this little dog could say and think of, so it felt for me like the whole conversation was about food and not about my orientation for my stay in this grand home.

"Why yes," this woman replied in a sweet tone, "and she loves her new food..." she told me happily.

I said, "Well, I'm not sure she likes the new food. It might be really nice for her if you went back to the old food."

I heard the dog say a very enthusiastic, 'Yes!'

Again my brand new host, who only knows of me through our mutual friends, I'm sure is thinking, 'What is going on here with this woman?' She says, "NO, I think she really likes her new food."

I hear the dog again, 'I don't like my new food.'

So I say gently, "I R-E-A-L-L-Y don't think she likes the new food." and, "She liked the old food better."

This lovely woman glared at me and changed the subject. A few sentences later she said she had to leave for work and that I should make myself at home. Now I knew she was thinking she had a crazy person in her home.

A few days passed. I had been leaving before she got up and

coming home after they had gone to bed (the dog slept with her). On about the fourth evening when I walked into the house, she and the dog were still up. There was a small gathering in her dining area with another mutual friend of ours, plus a woman I had hoped to meet; they were enjoying hors d'oeuvres and wine.

The dog was happily getting affection from all of the women in the room, and lovely conversation and fun stories were being shared. I felt very welcomed and all of the strangeness that I was carrying about our first meeting dissolved.

We all chatted, laughed and ate... Then the owner looked at me and said, "Remember how you talked to me about her food?" 'How could I forget?' I thought, 'and here it comes'... I nodded. She said, "Well as if to make a point after you mentioning this to me, she has been putting the red bits of the food everywhere. I have found them in these chairs," she pointed to what she was sitting on, "in the sofa over there, on the floor, and even buried deep in the covers of the bed which are white! So I switched her back to her old food."

I was laughing inside; this dog had some talent. I smiled and nodded on the outside, winked at the dog, and the night's conversation went on to many other things, none of which were about the dog's food. We looked at all the amazing photos she had taken of the dog in different environments that she would send to friends to make them smile.

The next few days passed and it was time for me to leave. I had become accustomed to talking to the horses and dogs daily that lived outside at this home, but I did not have contact with my little food friend as she was always in the company of her owner.

As I was saying my thank you and goodbyes, this well bred-lady looked me in the eye and said, "Before you leave, does my dog have anything else she wants to tell me?"

I was stunned. I looked at the little dog at her feet who was looking up at me and said, "I don't know, let me ask her." I asked internally, the way you talk to dogs, and the little dog said 'No, just the food.' So I told her owner, "Nope, her only complaint was about the food."

She smiled and said, "Good." I nodded and thanked her once again, in the wonder of it all.

Blessing:

I love that this dog and other animals have been pushy with me to tell their story. I have gotten better with my gifts over time. That said, it can still be a little hard for me in the 'real/(fake) world' where we have etiquette. These experiences put me in wonder, and I do wonder how many animals, loved or not loved and anywhere in-between, are not 'heard' for whatever they are wishing to tell us. No matter how much we love them, we are often sure we know what is best for them and that they don't know for themselves, or if they did they are only animals, even though they are our beloveds.

So powerful that this little one had only one complaint, only wanted ONE change; how many of us could say that? 'Please grant my one (small) request and I will return to my 100% happy rating in my life. I had only dropped to 99%, but change this and I am back to 100%!' This little gal was a deep blessing in once again sharing the world in which I live, see, and hear.

Offering:

Is there an animal near you that is trying to tell you something? If you quieted yourself, what are they trying to say? And how would you behave once you had this information? What would it change for them and you?

GUIDANCE FROM A
NATIVE AMERICAN ELDER

Shortly after I first moved to Arizona, I thought God was mad at me.

I had lived and practiced in the most affluent area in Pennsylvania for many years. The children at the school that my daughter attended were rewarded when they graduated from high school with a Mercedes or a Jaguar as a graduation gift. All of them. At one moment, one girl who was under my care, was so distressed that her father bought her an expensive car for her graduation gift but it was a few years old and not new. In our community the message this sent to her was that she wasn't good enough. This was a very painful moment for all of us, as we believed this was not at all the message her dad meant to convey, but in this community it could, and most likely would, be taken this way.

So, here I landed in rural, poor, Northern Arizona, the complete opposite of what my life had been. God must be angry with me.

Day after day I wondered what I had done wrong, what I was being punished for, why and for how long this would last. I was beginning to believe that it wasn't going to end.

It seemed that God was silent, causing me to believe even more strongly that I was being excommunicated and that I was all alone to pay my penance for something I couldn't understand I had done to cause this.

As I have shared, I had been adopted by a Native American family and had started some of my trainings in that world, then my family disappeared. They had warned me that this might happen as they were planning to attend a ceremony that was very controversial and still outlawed. They told me if I didn't hear from them, that something bad had happened as they would always find me and be in touch with me if all was well. Time had passed and I was not knowing what to think or feel about all of this; I just felt very lost and sad, as if everyone and everything had left me, including God.

In the small town where I lived there was a beautiful Native elder. She was elegant and full of dignity and pride, it seemed to me. When I watched her she seemed full of wisdom so I decided to try to speak to her. I had tried on two occasions to quietly request to understand what I needed to do to have an audience with her. Trying to understand the honor, prayers and traditions I needed to do in order to ask a question or to be honored to be guided by her.

She ignored me all of the times I was around her. No matter what I did or didn't do, she ignored me. This seemed to make my isolation go to the bone. I had my children and husband, but I felt more alone than ever in this beautiful, mystical area in Arizona.

I finally decided after much angst that I would write one question down for her and give it to a friend of hers and ask this friend to deliver it to her. I wrote something like this, 'I am the woman who has been trying to speak to you. I was adopted by a Native family, who now seem to have disappeared. I was hoping you might share your wisdom with me and answer one question for me. Why am I here? Why has Great Spirit brought me here?' I signed my name and folded it in half, with the friend promising to deliver the paper to her Native friend; no promises about a response.

Months passed and I would see this Native woman frequently in the little town outside of which we lived. She continued to act as if she didn't see me, ever.

I started to completely give up. I knew that she had received my note as her friend told me she had given it to her, and that she had read it in front of her. I had nowhere else to turn. I was thinking all of the magic in my life, all of the miracles I had experienced, all of the connection with all of life I felt was gone, and without it I wondered if this was how 'normal' people felt, and if it was, no wonder people were so sad and mad. There was no wonder in their lives and now my life as well.

I was haunted by the words of a dear friend who had done body work on me not long before I had left the East Coast for Arizona. He said the work he was doing was balancing me and much-needed but that I would probably lose my abilities, my psychic and all of my other abilities, and that I needed this balancing very much so it would be worth it.

I laughed at the time, thinking there was no way could he change me that much. This was a part of my Soul's talents, and no matter how much I had tried to get rid of it when I was younger, all these years later it was a deep part of my life; a usual part, talking to trees and rocks and birds and streams, much of the time knowing or hearing them speak but even more frequently knowing things I shouldn't or wouldn't know if they hadn't shared with me their points of views and stories.

Now all of this seemed a frightening shadow of my past and not really a part of my future. Who do you go to when you lose your way like this but a Native healer? It turned out that was exactly what she was but I would not find that out until much later.

Days, weeks and months passed. I had given up and was barely living inside of myself. Yes I was doing all of the daily things: talking, taking care of the kids, admiring the blue sky every day, existing in my body with no real connection, where I thought I should feel deeply connected. It was the West after all.

Then one day, I was in town, in a new friend's shop, and there she was. I politely ignored her. Not in a mean shunning way, but in a polite, 'I understand, I am not part of your world' way, the way I was taught by my Native family to honor an elder that I did not know. So I felt no tug inside. I understood that she was not going to help me and I had become neutral with that, maybe even seeking the lesson she was giving me though this teaching of not including me.

I was calm. We went about our ways in this little shop, and I became fascinated by something, when suddenly she was there in front of me, face right in front of me. Looking directly in my eyes she said, "SO! You.. Want to know.... Why you are here?"

I was stunned. I had never heard her speak and her voice

was filled with power. "Yes," I said meekly after I gathered my thoughts.

She looked deeply into my eyes again, holding on to me. I felt I couldn't move or blink. She had me. Then she said, and I will never forget it, "Great Spirit has brought you and your family HERE so that when the earth changes come you and your family will be safe." And she walked away.

This was to be the beginning of an amazing story between she and my family. She would later teach me and mentor me to become a medicine woman through her lineage and wisdom. But in that moment and for sometime after, this would be the gift she would leave me to ponder with wonder and joy.

In my aloneness with this dear beloved message from the Great One, my gifts returned on their own, seeming to be more powerful and power-filled than ever.

Blessing:

Confirmation that I was in fact in the right place where Great Spirit wanted me, even though it didn't feel that way. An awareness that everything (and everyone) has its time and timing and to honor that, no matter how it is feeling. Being with uncomfortable and empty feelings; ones that for me had no direction to take action, were difficult to be with, as it is my nature to overact, to be busy, to be in some sort of physical action, as opposed to the wait where things can be healed, reoriented, reorganized and cleaned up for the next level of work or learning, or giving and receiving.

This was a powerful lesson in so many ways. And would be

one of many that I would learn later being taught traditional Native Lakota ways, by this amazing and powerful woman.

Offering:

Be patient where you might be anxious. The gifts that you are to receive and the work and path that you are to take may not be prepared yet, or you may not be prepared yet. Take the time to trust and continue to hold out your hands and keep your heart open for what the Great One has in store for you.

FALLING IN LOVE
WITH A PACK RAT

I was living in a cabin years ago that was, to me, a wondrous and magical place, but to others it was viewed as a shanty.

I loved it. It was in the middle of nowhere, where the outside seemed part of the inside. I was miles off-the-grid, the closest neighbor about a half-mile away who was doing the same as I, living closer to the earth.

It was wood for heat and hauling water, again, my paradise. So when the opportunity came to return to living in this cabin and this life for a while with my son and boyfriend, I, with great excitement, dragged them with me to my heaven. (Keep in mind this was and is MY heaven. For my son and Wayne, not so much.)

I happily packed up everything I owned and started to make my way back to the place I have always felt like a true home for me. I was overjoyed that everyone seemed to be going along with this idea, even if not completely on board with it.

We arrived at the cabin which had been abandoned for years. I had visited it on and off but it seemed that people who had come upon it over the years had left their damage and some critters also had made it their home. Overjoyed, I saw none of this as an issue. I was going to be able to live for a handful of months in this place that nurtured my soul, with my dear son and beloved Wayne and animals I loved. What could be better?

Wayne and Conner were anything but enchanted. We had to charge phones in the car as there was no indoor electricity. The rats and mice had eaten the little electrical wiring that had been in the cabin. I loved it that we were on candle light every night. There was no indoor running water. I loved taking a bath outside under the moonlight in a cast iron bathtub that we would build a fire under. No television. I loved all of us watching a movie with the generator going and making popcorn, all sitting together.

This cabin had many doors and windows. I loved that my horses could put their heads in the windows and wake us up by sticking their heads in the one over our bed. I loved that my horses could come in the house and be with us inside the house, even when the wood stove that heated the cabin was burning. I loved that I kept fruit on the kitchen table in a big bowl. I loved that on occasion the horses would choose some fruit and take it out of the bowl and eat it as we would. I felt so much joy at what felt like my private Dr. Dolittle home.

I loved one day walking in my son's room and finding a young draft horse that we have, her hooves pushed under his bed, her head over his as he slept. She had her nose almost touching his face, as if she were waiting for him to wake up and play with her. I loved everything. We had an eighty-five pound tortoise that lived in our home, kitties, and a rabbit too.

This was everything I dreamed, but not for my son and Wayne. They were very kind to me about the passion I had for this life, but the line they drew was about the pack rats. As I said, there were rats and mice that had moved in when I was gone and they really wanted to maintain their penthouse, and I being an honorer of all life was at a crossroads.

The little creatures were somewhat kind to us and tried to stay, for the most part, out of view, although we would see them and the pack rats would build these crazy nests. I agreed we would dismantle and try to move these nests or encourage their inhabitants to move to a better location. Wayne, and occasionally I, had been continuously dismantling these homes.

I was starting to feel that one rat in particular was very beautiful and feminine. Her homes were made with such art, to me, and she seemed to want to nest in a corner of the cabin that was where we had moved our bed when I wanted to be closer to the wood-burning stove. Days would pass and these magnificent nests would appear. It got to the point that I couldn't take them apart and would ask Wayne to move them.

Then the day came when my love for this rat and her life and home took over. I was cleaning and came upon her nest, close to the usual spot. I exhaled. 'Not again,' I thought. I just hated to dismantle these homes. Yes, they are rats... But aren't we also? We destroy so many things, too. Without them, the world to which we add garbage would have been destroyed by us long ago, as they help destroy and break down things so the earth can take them back and keep her balance.

So I crawled under the bed, preparing myself to take her home apart. Instead my breath was taken away in a beautiful way. There at her home this little rat had found small pieces from my daughter's life when she was a little girl and built them into her home. I remembered the original items and how my daughter had lived or played with these objects that now were, in their destruction, made so beautiful again by the clear intention of their placement in this little home.

I smiled, and laughed, and cried. I really felt I loved this rat. I loved her eye, her sense of design. I loved that she loved and was attracted to the things my daughter had loved and had lovingly found them in some garbage pile and brought them back to life as a beautiful, eye-catching decoration in her home.

I spoke to her home, I had no idea where she was. I told her I was her, trying to make a home in a hovel. I told her we could share this place together and really there was no difference in her, or the cat, or the rabbit, or me.

Once again, there is nothing outside of me; nothing that the Divine puts in my path that is outside of me. This little rat held for me all of my dreams of what I wanted this cabin/home/hovel to be for my family. This included the tiny little fresh yellow flower she had placed next to the opening for the door.

Blessing:

What a deep and powerful gift to fall in love with something you are supposed to hate and kill and keep killing, exterminating. I have never hated them or wished to kill them.

However, I have been taught that you are not a fit human being if you have a rat or rats in your house. I have always been an odd one this way, somehow always feeling very comfortable around 'wild' animals. As a child I would carry them home and even now have had the occasional touch with them. I cannot see their evilness or all of the stories we have put in them. Without this bunch the planet would not have survived, they are part of an amazing, intricate system that keeps us all well and balanced.

All of this said, when I felt my heart jump as I saw the beauty in her nest and her care, I could see her as me. I could see me though her. I have always loved the look of the pack rats here in Arizona. To me they look like personalized miniature Disney characters. They are really adorable and seem to also have a bit of wisdom.

For me to have the honor to live with her in this little corner of my human pack rat house was a gift; one that perhaps many of you will not understand, but for me, I even started to look forward to changes in her decorations and the feeling I was a cohabitant with all on the planet. As if, for the first time I had been accepted, was not an outsider anymore, that I was one with the bigger community that has its honored place and job to help our planet Earth.

Offering:

If there are critters with which you are really struggling, try to look at what they are offering or what they are doing for you, or the gift they are trying to give to you. Take a thought-filled perspective, one that you have thought through and not one that is just a given, or default. Much of what is happening to our Mother Earth and all of her creatures, I believe, is happening because we are not challenging beliefs that do not benefit our earth and all of us. Each of us is deeply interwoven and in need of each other; from bacteria, to plants, to trees, soil, air, water, insects, rodents, animals, birds, reptiles and more. All are pieces that cannot be lost.

As amazing as it might seem to us humans, we all are equal, even though we do not behave this way. We have added little towards our sister and brother animals and insect, reptile, all other beings on the planet. We have really only taken from them more recently from a very entitled standpoint. So, love in Grace and honor. See it from their point of view and give something to them, even if it is relocation with love.

DOWSING FOR LOST THINGS

When my daughter was young she was accustomed to me using non-traditional methods to solve daily problems. We would always solve problems in ways that worked for us, hence the dowsing rods.

On at least two occasions, we were up against the wall to find items immediately. The first was a library book that was long, long overdue. We had been scouring the house for months and months looking for this book and we had turned the house upside down looking for it. It was now months overdue and I was out of options. So my daughter, then maybe age six, and I got out the dowsing rods, which were two wire coat hangers bent into an L-shape.

We held the image of the book in our minds and walked through the house. It started to cross (an indication that you are near or at the item you are seeking) under a ladder that went to an upstairs attic bedroom. We had a rabbit that was litter-trained and his litter box was behind this ladder on the floor next to the wall, that went into a downstairs bathroom.

When the dowsing rods crossed, Kaitlyn and I looked at each other. What? Where could this book be? I kept holding the rods and moving closer, my daughter and I thinking, 'Really? Is the library book really here? Really?' The closer we looked, it was, tucked behind the litter box, up against the wall, a similar color to the wall and completely behind this litter box. We would have NEVER found this book until we moved, as even though we were cleaning the box often, the way it was tucked behind it we never saw it. Victory for the dowsing rods!! My daughter and I danced and hooted and howled!

On another occasion my daughter and I were going to go on a trip to the Bahamas where she and I and my boyfriend were going scuba diving for a week. I was just learning to dive and was very involved in getting us ready for this trip and working, and, and, and. At the last moment my daughter couldn't find her bathing suit. We were leaving in only a few hours and we couldn't find her bathing suit.

I went through all of the crazy parent thoughts like, 'It's winter. Where could it have gone?' I think I checked all of her stuffed animals to see if one of them was wearing the suit. I was definitely wound up and I think my daughter said, "Mommy why don't you dowse to find it?" 'Silly Mommy I thought! Of course!' Out came the rods and within moments the suit was found and packed. Stress gone, onto the hugs and off to an amazing vacation.

A big thank you again to the amazing energies we often forget to use, that are here for us, to support us in every moment of our lives. We are in the hands of loving energy, always.

Blessing:

There is always help! This was my lesson. I tend to do every-thing on my own, without asking for help from anyone, including those who are assigned to help me, those who as just waiting for me to ask (in both physical and non-physical bodies), Angels, God who is always patient, on and on.

I have a tendency to think, "No, it's OK, when it gets REALLY bad I'll ask but for now I'm not suffering too much so I'm good" What??? Really this is a planet of helpers; we have helper beings surrounding us all the time. Just ask!! Ask the spider, ask the dog, ask Saint Anthony or Saint Michael, or your Guardian Angel, your dead grandma, or anyone who has died including your deceased animals. Ask your pendulum, muscle testing or ask your dowsing rods, but, "Hey, Karen (was my message), ASK!" The rest is easy and nurturing and supportive and loving... But you must ask.

Offering:

Please, please, please... Ask.

DEATH

Many times we are so deeply sad, grieving, longing and wounded when a being loses its physical body. Sometimes it seems we never recover and that we carry this loss for the rest of the time we stay in our physical body in this lifetime.

When someone or something dies, a human or animal makes their transition, we often believe they are gone, and that we will need to wait until we die for us to see them again. This is not true. I often joke that our strongest prejudices aren't about people because of color or sex; our strongest prejudices are about those who have given up their bodies. We don't want to talk to anyone who has passed on, who has died, and truly they are still with us and in other places too, but with us the same as they were, person or animal, just without the body.

They are waiting, always waiting, to help us, love us, guide us and continue to be in relationships with us. We are the ones who have so many superstitions and tales about interacting with them. Yet we are so comfortable with God being a Spirit, invisible like the wind, and Angels, Christ, the Holy Ghost, the same; we are accustomed to praying and asking for guidance and help from these Great Spirits.

I know through experience over and over again that human and animal souls are ever-present in the Light and Love of God's being, for there is nothing that can be outside of the energy and love that is God stuff. We are all made of this stuff and so is everything that we live in and touch and all of the others that travel with us, human or otherwise. And this includes animals, the ones we call pets, the ones we see as birds, and in our daily day environment. The wild ones that we see and the ones we don't. The ones we eat. The trees, rocks, bugs are all part of us and are more than willing to help us and guide us with wisdom and grace. We just need to stop, ask and listen. Really listen for the answers that they are more than happy to give.

I have had trees give me directions and laugh with me when I asked them how it was for them to have an ugly plastic bag stuck in them. They said, 'People look at us a lot more!! It is funny to be noticed in this way, and hear people make their comments. We do hear your voice and thoughts. We are the standing ones, we watch you drive by us every day. We know and notice you, but you don't seem to notice us. We could teach you much. We are not separate from anyone, or anything.'

There is no way for you to be alone, and every thought is heard, every action felt. And truly all we need to do is know we are all of equal energy, we are all related; rock, spiders trees, earth, wind, those who have no bodies, mountains, animals, all dead, dying and alive. All those you eat including the plant people. The stars and all; talk to all of them, ask questions, learn to listen for how they will answer back.

Be free and feel loved. This is your story. These are all our stories. Be kind as there are no enemies and what you hurt is yourself. These stories we write on our Souls. Truly there is only Love or the illusion of the separation from it. So find your way back to love. Find your way. And if you don't know your way back, ask a friend, a rock, a tree, a dog, a cloud. Ask for help and ask for your heart to heal. Ask that you will always remember who you are.

Blessing:

For me these experiences have been an incredible blessing and more of a reinforcement that our death date whether for human or animal is planned. I have really come to know that our death time and the way we die for animals and people is written before we arrive here on planet earth. This is a real comfort to not only know this as a fact, but also to be able to share this with the folks who are around the beloved one who passes. This seems deeply and especially true when a beloved one dies in what seems a sudden and tragic way, and there is the feeling that something could have been done to have prevented this death. Again, when I look at the idea that this would have happened no matter what, that it is part of that Soul's plan to leave this way, and we can find grace and honor and love for that beloved journey, somehow I believe it changes everything.

Offering:

Start being open to the idea that death is by a beloved's and our Soul's design; that there is no changing this, and that each Soul wishes to express and experience its leaving its body in different ways, ways that it writes on its Soul for the next time around. Try to send love and wonder to these deaths, and know that it is just leaving the body behind in a magical way (no matter how it seems), to its next adventure of wonder.

A DEAD GRANDFATHER
RETURNS TO HELP

I had a request from a dear friend of mine to see if I could help the son of a life-long friend of hers. This woman's son seemed to be daring life to keep him alive.

He was and had been involved with drugs and had a drug problem in his home country, so had gone to a foreign country to live. There he became deep into drugs again and had received death threats from the drug dealers with whom he was involved.

His mother had gone to the authorities and somehow had helped he and some of his possessions get out of the country. He was alive and now his mother wanted to know if I could be a last hope for helping her son. I was hopeful that there might be a driving force that had gone unknown until now.

We brought this young man to my friend's home, to her treatment room. Since he had grown up with my friend's boys and had spent much of his childhood time in this home, he knew everyone in the home. He also knew many of the people waiting in the home to see me.

He walked though the home's rooms and greeted everyone.

He entered the room where I was going to see him. Inside the room was also a dear friend of mine who would be doing the translation. This young man spoke perfect English, however, I wanted to do the session in his native language and for him to hear in all ways the words I would speak in the language he heard as a child.

So we began, with a bit of resistance on his side. He really wanted to show me how well he could translate and speak English and that he didn't need anyone else in the room. I convinced him that it was important and would be nice to hear things in both languages so that he could relax.

He was lying on a table and was very aware, I believe, of the stories that I had heard about his life. It seemed to me that he was doing this not completely for himself, so we chatted a bit about his life and dreams.

I asked him about his younger years. I said that I felt that he felt there was only one person who really understood him and loved him for who he was, and that this was a man – a grandfather it looked like. I was reading his energy and also getting a strong tug from the Heavens.

He said 'yes.' As a little boy he had spent every day with his grandfather and he knew his grandfather loved him very much and he loved his grandfather very, very much.

Since his grandfather's death, no one really understood him. He was destroyed when his grandfather died. This young man had been sitting at a table right in front of his grandfather when his grandfather died right in front of him. I believe he told me he was seven. I also believe he said he was alone with him when he died. He told me he really missed his grandfather, every day.

I asked if he would like to speak to his grandfather. I asked him if he would like to know how he was if it was possible for us to call his grandfather and said that we would have to ask the Angels for some help.

For the first time this young man's face seemed a little peaceful and he agreed. So I went about the process of asking if his grandfather could come and talk to this grandson who watched him die so long ago.

Before I had finished asking for his grandfather to come to us he had already shown up, and the grandson said to me, "He's here."

I encouraged him to take his time, ask as many questions as he wished, and to spend as much time with his grandfather as he wanted; to ask him to sit and talk and talk, to catch up, and if there had been any unsaid things, anything that he needed advice on, any pain that he was in, anything, that he could ask his grandfather for help. My friend Silvia was doing all of the translating at this time and we were both seeing changes in this young man's face.

I allowed for a very long, silent time for them to share together. After this time, I gently asked, "How are you doing?" This was translated in the soft tone I used, by Silvia. This young man resisted talking to me, so I gently, in a quiet voice again asked, "How are you doing?" This was again translated in a soft tone.

This man then said to me in a stern tone, "Please, you're interrupting our conversation every time you are talking to me." I told him I would be quiet and when he was finished he was to open his eyes and I would thank all the Spirits who made this possible.

After a long, quiet time of Silvia and I just winking and smiling and nodding silently at each other, he opened his eyes. He seemed transformed. I asked if there were anything else for me to do for he and his grandfather. He said there was not, thanked me deeply and was ready to leave.

He sat up, and truly, he looked like a completely different person.

I am not sure of the moment, but suddenly the room was filled with Light. Light! He appeared to be years younger and a different person, as if he had a different life story written all over him and behind him, and around him the room was filled with Light.

Silvia and I were making quiet gestures to affirm what we both were experiencing. We opened the door to the room and there were the same people sitting in the waiting area as before. This young man gently said his goodbyes to all in the room.

The husband/father of the home came in and this young man gave him a big hug and said a happy goodbye to him and made his way out the door. The husband looked at me with wonder and said, "Who was that young man?"

Sylvia and I couldn't believe that he didn't recognize him, as he was not only a long-time childhood friend of his sons, but he had greeted him just one hour ago. In fact, later the people in the room guessed it was him but they weren't sure. The husband of the home just would not, and could not, believe that this was the same person.

Silvia and I kept looking back at the bright Light still shining out from this healing room, now fading a bit, feeling

113

blessed to be a part of such an incredible experience.

Blessing:

This experience held many blessings for me:

How loved ones who have passed are always there with us, ready to help us, even if it has been years and years without contact or acknowledgement.

How a trauma like this from childhood can redirect one's life forever, since this deep love and understanding feels lost and not replaceable in any way. We travel with a huge open hole, feeling like it cannot ever be filled again (which is not true).

How instant healing or change can be.

For everyone to not recognize him, for who he had become was the one they really needed to not recognize, as he was not living in his Divineness, he had not been fully himself for a very long time.

How it really seems so simple, doesn't it? Just ask with an open heart for the REAL thing you need, and you might very well receive it, with grace, beauty, and glory, and much, much love and healing.

So, be ready.

Offering:

See if there is a wound in your life from which you can't seem to unhitch yourself. Start to make friends with it, as if it were your biggest gift (as it is and you just don't know it yet).

See what you need to heal, really need to heal, such as forgiveness, or sending love to the unlovable, or asking for help talking to a loved one who has passed and know that they are okay. Whatever it is, find the highest healing that you need, turn your wound into your strength and your gift, ask for what is left after that to be healed, and SHINE!

Then, run to do what you and the Divine have set up in this lifetime for the part only you can do, and SHINE more of your beautiful, Divine, Holy self. Bring more love and light, grace and compassion to the planet and all who live here.

CHA CHA AND VOLCOM,
BLESSED DOGS

We had bought a property in what seemed the middle of nowhere. For me this felt like a dream as I could feel my heart open more and more as we drove down the long dirt road home.

The sight of fewer and fewer homes and people along the way and more and more wildlife comforted me in ways to this day I cannot really explain, except to say that I feel deeply as if I have been returned 'back' with my true family.

The trees, rabbits, hawk, eagle, antelope, rock people, ants, spiders, flies, weeds, sky, sun, and on and on, all feel to me as if they are my teachers, family, friends and beyond as they feel the deepest, truest part of me. Living far away for others felt like living next door for me, to all of my dearest beloved ones.

One of these beautiful at-home days the family was all together doing things at the house which was a work in progress. My son was three at the time, my daughter about eleven. We were playing games in and out of the house as we were working and doing some building.

To me it was a magical day. I was in the midst of all of my

families in my wilderness, with all that I loved surrounding me. The light of the day was brilliant, warming and magnificent and everything around me felt illuminated. I remember taking a few moments to stop, look, and really breathe in how perfect this day felt to me.

Then, out of nowhere, this black lab-looking mommy dog and her blonde baby puppy showed up. As if out of thin air, they came trotting up our little hill and seemed to wish to visit and play. My children were ecstatic, especially my daughter who had been asking for a puppy for a long while.

We had gotten a puppy shortly after we moved to the property, that had died suddenly. We thought it was from some sort of poison but we really were not sure, so we had been waiting, just waiting, for what I am not sure. But we had been in a waiting time, a long waiting time with no end and no real reasoning behind this waiting.

So, the mom and puppy were with us and it really seemed that this mommy dog was seeking out my daughter. My son lost interest after a bit and it truly felt like this mommy dog was interacting only with Kaitlyn and sharing her only puppy with her.

This was so curious that I watched and watched and then would get pulled away, distracted to doing something else, then I would come back for brief moments of observing, thinking this was the most beautiful thing I had ever seen; these three playing together as a little girl group, laughing and playing, and the mommy continuing to watch how my daughter handled her baby.

This went on all day, and I do mean all day. It seems to me that country time is different from city time, that when we are at a distance from what we humans have created we can be more ourselves, closer or in our true nature, and we feel the timing of nature more deeply. Everything is slowed.

This day was a day like that, slow and intentional, easy and open. Time was carrying us in its hands on this day instead of us chasing after time and being pulled out of ourselves in the chase. So the day was long and wide and by nightfall the mommy dog and baby were still with us. They had stayed all day.

I was just starting to have the inner conversation about keeping them both, that our wait was over, when the mommy got up and left. It was as if she had chosen my daughter to receive her baby; as if in some way I could only try to understand she believed my daughter was the one who should continue the care for the only puppy we saw she had.

We called to her to come back and I believe she only looked back once over her left shoulder before she trotted back over the hill over which she had come to us many hours earlier.

We were stunned. My daughter did become the next best mommy to this baby girl dog who would be named Cha Cha. We never saw this mommy dog again, never in all the years we had lived there, and at some moment we became convinced that Cha Cha's dad had been a dog that had become ours who was part wolf.

Our Cha Cha spent a long life with us. In the end she really became the mother to us and the keeper of all our stories. She really raised us more than we raised her.

This story caused me to wonder even more deeply as years passed. Years later, my son and I left my husband and moved to an area in which we had not lived before. There was a stray dog known to all in the neighborhood. This dog would not stay with anyone, he had just wandered for years as far as we knew, visiting folks here and there but never staying.

This dog came to us one day, a stunning pit bull, handsome and kind, muscular and playful. My son and a friend had great fun playing with him. When evening came it seemed like it was going to be a cold night, as I remember, so I put this dog in a work shed on the property and we gave him food and a warm bed. I didn't care if he went to the bathroom in this shed as I was concerned that he shouldn't be out in the cold. In the morning we got up to let him out and he was gone. He had broken though a window and so was free to do as he pleased.

Months passed. Then one day my son and the same friend he had been playing with the day the pit bull came to visit were over at a neighbor's house. This neighbor cared for stray dogs and had many that he had adopted. The boys were hanging out when this same pit bull came from nowhere and started to play with them again, as if they were long-lost friends.

The man who helped the strays said this dog would come and visit, but never stay. He'd take a meal here and there, that he wished he could find the dog a home where he would stay, but he never stayed.

This time my son felt something different in this dog. I don't remember if they brought him back on a leash or if he just followed my son and his friend to our home.

Conner named this dog Volcom, after one of his favorite

skateboard companies. Somehow, in some way, Volcom must have chosen us, like that mommy dog chose Kaitlyn long ago.

Volcom has lived with us ever since. There have been many times he could have run away and not come back, but that has never happened. It seems that somehow he chose Conner to be loyal to and so the rest of the family.

To this day Volcom still chooses the love of this family, and daily I continue to be in wonder and gratefulness for his choice.

Blessing:

NEVER, never believe anything isn't possible with our animal companions. We really know so little about them and yet we think we know so much. I feel in the presence of any animal, including insects, that I am in front of a great Buddha teacher and that I must still myself and prepare to learn. Great gifts are everywhere; certainly everywhere in the Animal Kingdom.

Our Cha Cha died during the writing of this book, and even in her last day, last moments, she has been one of my greatest teachers – a mother to us all.

Offering:

Look deeper, open wider to the animals that live with you, call to you, and come to you. You never know what amazing gifts they have waiting for you.

YOU'VE RUINED MY LIFE

I had been invited to go and spend some time with a trainer who was taking a brand new approach to horses that were being trained at a race horse facility in Italy.

The new idea was to bring natural horsemanship to these young horses along with their usual training, hopefully to offer them a deeper understanding of what humans wanted from them in a more connected, calmer way. Then, for the ones who did not make it as racehorses, to have a lovely foundation for whatever their future job might be. This felt to me a very progressive idea, especially in rural Italy, and I was excited to see how these ideas were being implemented.

The trainer who was bringing this new idea to this facility also traveled to other facilities. He was training all of the trainers who worked with the horses daily. This man, who was not Italian but lived in Italy, was fluent in a few languages and the trainers who worked with these horses daily might have understood and spoken English, my native language, but were waiting for translation as they were very interested in me and my experiences.

We toured the facility which really was beautiful, AND horse friendly, as many are beautiful to the human eye but have absolutely no room or understanding about the horses themselves or how they function and really need to live and be cared for. Horses have given us so very much in how they adapt to us and our needs, very often being pushed far beyond the limits of their innate design by our strange human ideas of who and what they should be and do and how they should live.

This facility seemed to know horses. The owner realized their need to be together, to be able to move freely in huge spaces to exercise their bodies and minds, to be treated with respect and honor. The horses were watched for their abilities, knowing that every horse would not be a racer, even with the best breeding. Again, this seemed a very rare gift to me as the horse industry is just that: an industry that can be brutal.

As I relaxed more and more at the openness of the daily trainers and what this new trainer had brought to this facility, I asked if I could walk around a bit more. I was excited by the new trainer and an old hand of a trainer who seemed to be listening to my every word. He was very, very skeptical and often seemed to argue a bit when the translation was being given to him of what I had said. So as we strolled he walked a bit behind as the natural trainer and I talked of many things.

As I was being shown the young mares, I was shown one who was having some body problems. After just a glance at her I knew I had to offer to help her. I asked if, with the small amount of time left, I could please see if I could give her some healing touch and energy. 'Yes' was the answer, as they had tried as many traditional things as they knew to do. I said it would be a gift for all they had shared with me, and got started.

The old trainer was quiet. A completely different energy was coming from him. I was surprised as voices hushed as I worked my prayers, energy and magic on this horse.

The older trainer stood at the horse's tail and started looking like he was seeing something fantastic. He started asking me questions very quickly and when our translator did not get the translation exactly right, the old trainer would correct him and say it exactly as he wanted in English! This was fantastic because I knew enough Italian that somehow I, too, picked up on the translation errors. The poor natural trainer was being caught in a conversation that he couldn't grasp or understand or be a part of, because the old trainer was SEEING colors coming off this young mare as I was working on her; colors that he had never seen before – Aura.

He was very excited at what he was seeing and asked for the translation, and when the natural trainer translated the word yellow as green, the old trainer and I both shouted "No! Yellow! Not green!" Poor guy! The old trainer was so frustrated that he said to me in English, "It is yellow coming off and around her stomach, yes?!"

The natural trainer said, "What?? I don't see anything. Show me. I can't see it. Why can't I see it and he can?"

The old trainer smiled. "Yellow," he said in English, and then shook his head as the natural trainer was still trying to figure out what was happening.

I knew something profound and Divine had happened for this mare and her daily trainer. Soon, I was finished and the mare seemed much more comfortable and walked in a completely different way, her body and soul seemed relieved of what had been of such discomfort and disconnection.

Then it was time for me to start on the long journey back to Rome, so we walked back to the several-hundred-year-old building that was the center for breaks and meals. The old trainer seemed bound in thought, while the natural trainer seemed confused and disappointed that he did not see anything of what I had done energetically.

I started to make my goodbyes, when the old trainer spoke to me in perfect English. He said, "What I saw, the yellow coming off that horse, I have never seen before. You have ruined my whole life. Everything I believed up until this point I will have to think about and change. I am not so happy about this as I had organized my life in a way I was very happy with, but now I must change because I have seen this. I don't like this at all... But thank you."

He smiled at me, shook his head, said a proper Italian goodbye and sat down on the step of this ancient building, a step on which I imagined many a life moment had been contemplated. He lit a cigarette and seemed to draw his Light inward, as I imagined he was already starting to remap his life.

Blessing:

It was so great for me to share this experience with another human being. Often when these things happen it is only me or sometimes someone in my family who shares what I see or feel. Even though it totally turned this man's world upside down (and isn't that why we are here, to experience and explore such things?), it was fun to have someone's other sense or senses open.

I believe we all possess these qualities and that we all spend a lot of time NOT sensing, instead of just being our natural selves and developing these senses over time.

Offering:

In your daily life try to open to something bigger all around you. Be confident and peace-filled. Like the dog who hears much more than we do, and smells much much more than we do, the world beyond our senses is there available and very real. Just open that you might experience some or a little of our world and its many many wondrous things happening just a bit outside of your more commonly over-used senses and pay more attention to your underdeveloped senses. And let's just see, smell, feel, sense, touch, hear what might be happening in your world.

MIND READING

My husband and I were buying a new home and the property was in escrow. One day shortly before we were to close on the property, my husband, my son and I drove past it, excited to be seeing it and knowing soon it would be ours.

As we drove by, we saw people on the property with a truck, loading wood and other things that were on the property – our property. We were a bit shocked to see this and all of us started to say what we felt we should do about this. The property is in an area where it would take a Sheriff at least an hour to come, so we decided to confront these folks ourselves and see exactly what they were doing.

When we drove up to the people I let Wayne handle the situation, as he can be very foreboding. It was a concern of mine that they might be confrontational if, in fact, they were caught stealing.

Upon Wayne's statement which was something like, "What are you doing here? We are the new owners of this property and the property is closing in three days to us." These folks told us that friends of theirs had been told they could come and take anything off the property they wanted. (We had been noticing other valuable items had been disappearing from the property even though the gates had been locked.) Wayne had been calmly handling the situation as we sat in our truck. My son was quiet but alert, by my side.

Suddenly I started to become very agitated with what they were saying, as if a fire was lit within me which is not my nature at all. I leaned in front of Wayne and said that they knew they were lying!

I told them that they needed to put all of the things that they had taken back, that they knew they were untrue as to anything they had said to us, that they were not hired to clean up the property and that they were taking advantage of the fact that no one had been there, they knew it was for sale, and they thought they could get away with this and they could not, and did we need to report their behavior to the Sheriff, and that we all would sit here and wait for the Sheriff to come so they could tell them their lie.

Wow! I don't ever recall behaving in this way, especially since Wayne had it handled. They consulted with each other and decided to unload their truck and we waited until they had done this (they were fast!), then we all left together.

As we were driving away, I started saying to Wayne and Conner that I couldn't believe what they had said. I went on and on about all the things they had said to us. I was on a roll and Wayne and Conner seemed to not be chiming in and saying, Yes, I can't believe that, too!" Instead, they were silent.

Finally I stopped and Wayne said quietly to me, "Doll, they didn't say any of that."

"What?" I said, "Yes they did! Didn't you hear them say..."

And again, I went on.

Wayne again, very patient with me, said, "No."

Then Conner as well, "Mom, they didn't say those things. They were saying other things like..."

We were all silent for a while until Wayne said, "Doll maybe you were not hearing what they said but what they were actually thinking. Maybe you heard their thoughts." Then he went on to say he had observed this many times with me, that I would say someone said something that they never said. He wondered if all along I had just been hearing what they were actually thinking instead of what their mouths were saying. Conner agreed.

I was shocked. I had no idea that all of my life this might be so and now I know it is, the world I live in, hearing the truth of what people are thinking and not saying (and maybe all of life). This was a shock to learn that my world is so different than those experiencing it next to me and that my world has probably always been this way.

Blessing:

This caused me to look at everything from a new point of view... Everything! I love it when this happens!

Others have told me they hate it when this happens, but for me it is like a huge surge forward without much effort, that opens up new worlds and yes, we need to adjust many of the beliefs in our life surrounding this change, but Wow! It is so awesome to have shifts like this. It's like coming home and someone has moved your house to a place you could have only dreamed and the new space is really yours!!!

Learning about this piece of myself that I didn't even know and didn't know others were not operating from; this perspective was like a brand new beach-front property for me. I felt honored and graced and gifted that these two beloved beings would do this for me and give me this amazing gift. I hope there are more!

Offering:

Ask safe loved ones if there is anything they notice about you that you might not know about yourself. Ask if there are any habits and behaviors that they have observed or might even tease about (behind your back) that you might not know or of which you might not be fully aware, that could really change your life, or start a change if you knew about them.

Then enjoy, even more, the uniqueness of who you are.

GHOSTS

When I was a newbie in Chiropractic school a room became available in what was fondly referred to as the White House. This was a house which was over two-hundred years old near the school I was attending that had been a part of the underground railroad in Pennsylvania.

Two other Chiropractic students were already in this huge old house, that at some moment in its life had been divided with a giant wall down its center to create two huge living spaces. I moved into the student side with the two students, and a single mom lived on the other side of the huge wall that rose up through every story of the house.

My two fellow roommates warned me about the White House being haunted and that one ghost in particular would try for a few days to scare me, until it got accustomed to me being there. So it would take some getting used to being there.

This house must have been majestic in its day in a beautiful ancient wooden way, with two upstairs second floor bedrooms, a long hall, a bathroom at one end, an attic bedroom at the other, with a huge kitchen/dining area and living room downstairs.

This ghost was very well-known in the house by all who

had ever rented on the student side. My one roommate said, "Don't worry, it will only be a few days of him trying to get you gone and then he will get used to you and leave you alone. He won't harm you."

As I had had crazy things already happen to me in my life, I really thought nothing, and I mean nothing, of it. I didn't even think, 'Okay, we have an invisible roommate.' No, I just thought 'Okay, whatever,' and moved right in.

My room was the first bedroom at the top of the amazing enormous staircase next to the only, small bathroom on the student side of the house. My bedroom faced a busy street which I am sure was a narrow dirt road two-hundred years ago.

The day and evening I moved in, both of my roommates were gone and would be for the entire weekend. The single mom that was living next door was also gone, so I was all alone in the house. I just thought, 'Okay no problem, I will figure out where all the lights are and how it all works on my own.'

I had only one room of stuff at the time and it fit in the tiny room nicely so by evening I was officially moved in. Exhausted, I closed the door, quieted the house and turned off the light to go to sleep.

I exhaled and had completely forgotten (no, didn't even really think) about the ghost... Until I heard heavy foot-steps coming down the hallway, as if someone from the attic bedroom were coming to my room.

'Hmmm,' I thought, 'I wonder if one of my roommates came home and is going to come in and say "Hi.":...

Then it happened again, over and over, creepier and creepier. The steps started at the far end of the hall, then heavy and determined, walked to my door, stopping right at the door. Sadly, I must be a bit dense because it really took me a bit to figure out 'Oh! This is the ghost. I am being tested or he is trying to scare me. Right!' I was warned. I chuckled to myself... 'Okay, here we go... I must endure this.'

So in the pause between him stopping at my door and going back to the opposite end of the hall, I got up and turned on the hall light. 'There,' I thought, 'you probably will stop now since the hall is lit,' then I closed my door again.

There was a pause, then the walking started again and somehow now, to have seen nothing in the hall with the light on and the steps starting again, I knew he was 'out there.' How dumb is that, as 'out there' for a ghost is anywhere. But I wasn't thinking like that at our first meeting.

The walking continued and I started to get scared. What was I thinking to move in today when no one else is here. He might really be mad now. I called a friend (I had had the phone turned on in my room before I arrived) and talked to her about the ghost. Before long we were laughing and I hung up.

The steps would start and stop now, like he was getting the hang of how to scare me. So I thought, 'Okay now I'm really exhausted. I am a deep sleeper so I'll just go to sleep and know nothing and deal with this in the morning.' So off to sleep I fell... Until I had another experience.

I don't think I have ever been so terrified in all of my life. I woke up, not being able to breathe. There was a huge darkness in the room and something so heavy and crushing was on my chest that I was truly feeling like I was being killed by something I could not see but only sense.

I was unable to move or breathe and as I began to be struck by the fact that a ghost might kill me, I was reeling with thoughts like, 'How do I fight this? I have no idea.' No amount of struggling in the physical was relieving this.

Then, I saw my dad; my dead dad with some light around him. He was there right in front of me, arms open like a beautiful corridor with a beautiful garden behind him. Like a doorway, it was dark around him, like he was coming from his 'heavenly' world into my crazy dark ghost moment to do something.

I hadn't seen my dad in years. He looked young and smelled like 'Daddy' always did. He was warm and everything he always had been: loving, rescuing and happy. He grabbed me into his arms, hugged me and just stayed with me. He told me he loved me and it would be okay.

Now I wanted to stay with him. I had forgotten how powerful it was to smell him and be hugged by him. It was so great as I hadn't felt him hug me in my adult body; only my eleven-year-old one before he passed and so I didn't want this to end, ever!

But he somehow let me go and let me know all would be well. He surrounded me with love and then I was back in the dark room, breathing and alright. What? I turned on the light wanting to believe I was dreaming, however my body hurt and everything I just experienced was more real than anything I had seen or felt in years.

I sat quietly with the light on in my room, then the footsteps started again. Terror flew through my body, 'They said he wouldn't hurt me!' I heard myself scream inside. I called the same friend back and asked her to stay on the phone with me until the sun came up.

The house was haunted by many ghosts it turned out. Several passed through with a repeating theme.

There was a plantation-looking couple who floated through the huge wall that cut the house in two. Rich and happy, they looked like they 'danced' through the wall in their finest attire. I suspected they had much fine attire.

This became a bit of a game with the animals owned by us students and the single mom on the other side of the wall. We would phone each other when all the dogs and cats would watch the invisible somethings traveling through and along the wall that divided the house. It was crazy how the dogs and cats would line up next to each other in a proper line, heads moving all in unison, back and forth, up and down, all around, for many minutes at a time as if they all, on both sides of the wall were hypnotized and being directed by other worldly things and beings.

One afternoon, my roommate, Diane, was downstairs in the kitchen and yelled up the stairs, "Do you want anything?" This was a common thing in this house as we all seemed to go up and down the stairs a hundred times a day. "There are some really nice oranges, would you like one?"

"Sure," I yelled from my room (remember it was the one closest to the top of the staircase on the second floor). I walked out of my room to see the most perfect orange tucked at the top of the stairs where the staircase ended. Wow! I thought, she is really fast and I didn't even hear her walk up the stairs! "Thanks," I yelled down the stairs.

"What?" my roommate said. 'Hmmm,' I thought. 'She should know I am thanking her for delivering the MOST beautiful orange I might have ever seen.'

"For the orange!" I said.

"What?" she said, "What are you talking about?" Irritated, she said, "I haven't even gotten it for you yet, I am still doing clean-up down here. I'll bring it when I come back up."

I was stunned. Quiet. She was waiting for a reply. I called her name to come and look.

Irritated, she came up the stairs. We stared at the orange in silence. Then she said, "Well, now I don't have to bring you one!" and walked back down the stairs.

I thanked what I perceived was my walking trickster ghost, smiled, and ate the most yummy orange I had ever eaten!

Then there was the old black woman who sat in the living room near the kitchen. She just sat there. She seemed ancient, worn out, but content, happy; a life spent in a very hard place. She seemed to just be resting awhile and sat right above the huge, now 'earthed in' opening that was part of the underground railroad.

Occasionally we would see her in the kitchen but most of the time she sat in the living room. The dogs and cats seemed accustomed to her, maybe because she didn't seem to be 'visiting' like the fancy plantation couple. So they would usually stop, sniff and look at her and walk on by. Any time we would all sit together in the living room, if we saw her sitting in 'her' chair, none of us would sit in her chair, we'd just sit in the empty chairs or on the floor around her.

This all seemed to be how living in this ghost-filled house worked. After my father intervening from the side of Light it all seemed to be part of our day-to-day life; dogs and cats watching ghosts we did or did not see, the old woman happily resting in our living space, and then there were moments that shook me even deeper.

Like the matter of my roommate's paperwork; the roommate who lived in the attic. We worked for the same cable company as they were great about fitting work hours around school hours.

She was at work and had forgotten some paperwork that I could help get to her. She told me exactly where she had left it on her bed – easy!

So up in the highest part of the house I went. I always found her room a bit creepy, like every dark spirit or memory of the house lived there, and maybe they did. We knew where the underground railroad connected and there was another home far away, that was ironically owned by chiropractors, and was at the other end of one of the journeys the slaves were making.

So up the narrow attic stairs I crept, happy that it was afternoon and there was a lot of light going up to the room, although the room was always dark and cold. It was creepy enough that my roommate's young niece wouldn't go up into it, like never, like screaming never.

So I expected to see the paperwork on the edge of the bed, easily seen from the second to the top stair step, but no. Nothing. I think I audibly groaned as I REALLY did not want to move, not one more step into this cold and creepy room that really felt I was 'held' out of.

But I did. I walked around the two small rooms of the attic bedroom and looked everywhere, without touching anything. I was becoming convinced that my roommate had the paperwork somewhere else. Exasperated I said out loud, "I am here because of Diana. She needs her paperwork." I turned around and the paperwork was at the corner of the bed exactly where I should have been able to find it from the second from the top step.

I exhaled. "Thank you," I said, with a bit of sarcasm as I recall.

I grabbed the paperwork and started down the attic stairs. When I stepped down on that second step where I had stopped when coming up the stairs, I felt two hands clearly (and notably warmly) placed on my shoulders from behind. Before I could respond in any way (again, what do you do when a ghost touches/places his hands on you?) I felt the shove.

I clearly felt two warm/hot, really defined, open hands. I felt every finger and both palms, and then the SHOVE.

It was if I were pushed straight forward, strange, like pushed not down the stairs but off the stairs, away from gravity. It was a bit like flying forward until my gravitational pull took hold. It was a definite 'get out of here' shove.

I flew forward and then down. I remember seeing a Richard Bach quote my roommate had on the doorway wall at the uppermost part of the opening to the attic floor, "There is no such thing as a problem without a gift for you in its hands – you seek problems because you need their gifts."

Pondering the quote as an irony in my current (very bad) situation, I knew I was 'flying' too fast to catch my balance and prepared to be really injured, looking down at the old stairs and the famous hallway where the footsteps started when I first moved in.

I felt that I might end up on the floor face first, so I prepared, wondering how long I would be out of school with whatever would be broken, including pieces of my face.

Then suddenly I was uprighted and my feet placed on the floor firm and steady, paperwork still in hand, a bit disoriented. "Okay," I said, "Got the paperwork, won't do that again. I WON'T go up there and bother you again. I promise."

That said, my room remained haunted. I'm not sure if I ever asked if anyone else had happenings in their rooms. I think, again, it just became part of life in this house, natural and normal, that unseen beings were also living their lives and doing whatever they were doing along with us overwhelmed students.

Studying one evening for a critical life-or-death, hang-every-moment-of-your-future-on-it test (turns out they all are this way in DC school), I had my bed full, no, over-full with books and notes, stressing and cramming. My friend, the walking ghost, decided to distract me.

My old antique tin flour container full of clothing which probably weighed almost 100 pounds, started dancing across the floor. 'What??' Again my normal thinking, 'hmmm, must be a big truck or trucks driving by, causing this terrible vibration.' So I stopped studying, looked out the window, looked out the bedroom door, looked around. Nothing but a jumping tin, a jumping, dancing antique tin.

Irritated, I sat back down on the bed and pushed my head down and tried to study, tin still jumping, hopping visibly in the corner of my room. I was distracted. No matter how hard I tried I could not keep my focus on this life and career-threatening studying.

So I looked up, disgusted, and yelled, "Stop it! Just stop it! Can't you see I am trying to study??" ('Can't you see how important this is?' was the underlying message.)

It stopped immediately, never to jump or dance again.

Then I actually felt bad. I had been rude and demanding, not nice, and I never felt him again like this. Yes there was the occasional disappeared key or objects that reappeared quickly. But never again did I have a sense my 'friend' was playing with me.

Shortly and sadly thereafter I moved away from the beloved roommates who resided at the White House, only to tell their stories now and then. In some really crazy way I miss them all to this day.

Blessing:

I felt it was so amazing then, and now, to be able to live in a daily way with ghosts, not only to understand that they existed, but to start to understand them in their different dimensions, to actually have different types of relationships with them and to find honor and dignity for them in whatever their situations. There were some that just showed themselves and there were the ones who seemed aware of us humans and either wanted us to stay away from certain places, or the ones who wanted to be helpful, playful and noticed in some way.

For me to even contemplate any of this was a gift and continues to be whenever I reflect on these life experiences from any point of view that I continue to cultivate.

Offering:

Is there a place in your life that a bigger perspective or point of view could be taken?

After my rudeness to my personal ghost I realized how deeply my actions, reactions, judgements and options really affected others, including ghosts or those who might be in other dimensions.

What contemplation and change from that contemplation could you make to be kinder to all physical and non-physical beings?

In conclusion, never, never forget
how magical you are.

Never, never forget how magical all
of the beings are around you and how
wondrous the universe is.

Never, never forget that the Divine
is always conspiring FOR you, you are a divine
being of Light and Love, that God
is always wrapping you in miracles beyond
your wildest dreams.

Please always trust there is a
much bigger idea and plan of which
you are a precious part.

And Never, never, never forget
how much you are loved.

59338762R00089

Made in the USA
Lexington, KY
01 January 2017